MW01030406

BROKEN Open

EMBRACING HEARTACHE AND BETRAYAL
AS GATEWAYS TO UNCONDITIONAL LOVE

Published by Inspired Living Publishing, LLC.
P.O. Box 1149, Lakeville, MA 02347

Copyright ©Mal Duane 2019
All rights reserved.

No part of this publication may be reproduced, stored in a retrieval system, or transmitted in any form or by any means, electronic, mechanical, photocopying, recording, scanning, or otherwise, except as permitted under Section 107 or 108 of the 1976 United States Copyright Act, without the prior written permission of the publisher. Requests to publisher for permission should be addressed to the Permissions Department, Inspired Living Publishing, P.O. Box 1149, Lakeville, MA 02347 or by e-mail at Linda@InspiredLivingPublishing.com.

Limit of Liability/Disclaimer of Warranty: The Publisher makes no representation or warranties with respect to the accuracy or completeness of the contents of this work and specifically disclaims all warranties, including without limitation warranties of fitness for a particular purpose. No warranty may be created or extended by sales or promotional materials. The advice and strategies contained herein may not be suitable for every situation. This work is sold with the understanding that the Publisher is not engaged in rendering legal, accounting, counseling, or other professional services. If such assistance is required, the services of a competent professional should be sought. Neither the Publisher nor the Editor shall be liable for damages arising herefrom. The fact that an Author's organization or website is referred to in this work as a potential source of further information does not mean that the Publisher endorses the information the organization or website may provide, or recommendations it may make.

NOTE TO READERS: While the stories in this book are all real, true, and factual, names and identifying details have been changed to protect the innocent (and the guilty).

ISBN-13: 978-1-7327425-1-2
ISBN-10: 1-7327425-1-0

Library of Congress Control Number: 2019933085

InspiredLivingPublishing.com
(508) 265-7929

Cover and Layout Design: Brand Therapy, YourBrandTherapy.com

Editors: Bryna Haynes, TheHeartofWriting.com

Printed in the United States.

Dedication

THIS BOOK IS DEDICATED TO MY GREATEST TEACHER.

You inspired me to grow, to reach beyond my wildest dreams. You encouraged me to push the thin veil of illusion aside. Thanks to you, my spiritual practice has become my foundation for the structure of my life. I uncovered the glorious soul that had been hiding inside me, yearning to be expressed to the world as love.

Sometimes, the lessons you taught me were painful; ultimately, they left me broken open. But it was in those dark moments that I finally saw the incredible light that continues to guide me on this path of awakening and fulfilling my divine purpose.

The twisted, dark weed planted in the garden of your soul needed to emerge in order to be pulled. My fears and doubts of worthiness, which allowed me to dismiss it, needed to be healed.

An inevitable path of spiritual and personal transformation pulled us apart, but we were together for a reason.

I know our paths were meant to cross. Our stars were in alignment. We were brought together to heal those last, fragmented pieces in one another. Now, we know our work is complete, and there is nothing more we have to do for each other—at least, for now.

However, I know we have a connection that goes deeper than the love we have experienced on this physical plane; it will most likely follow us on to the next life.

Twin flame, your guidance is always welcomed. Your wisdom still inspires me. I believe our souls will meet once again in the cosmos where this unpredictable dance originated. Maybe we will even share one more tango.

A GIFT *for You*

Download Your

BROKEN *Open*
GUIDED JOURNAL

www.MalDuaneCoach.com/journal-gift

Praise for
BROKEN Open

"Mal Duane's *Broken Open* shows that finding wholeness, forgiveness, and unconditional love for yourself and others after your heart has been wounded by betrayal IS possible. Through storytelling and reflective self-inquiry questions, *Broken Open* guides women to see that the greatest source of love is their own brilliant heart. A must-read!"

CHRISTY WHITMAN,

New York Times best-selling author

"We are all recovering from something. Mal Duane, already a thought leader in the women's sobriety movement, has now provided a detailed roadmap for women in or seeking recovery from the heartbreak of betrayal. Mal has true compassion for women seeking healing in all areas of their lives - areas that she has healed (or is healing) in her own life. Always with compassion, Mal melds self-disclosure, memoir, and coaching to present women who have been hurt by betrayal both hope and practical guidance for moving forward. I'll recommend this book widely."

DAWN NICKEL, PHD,

Founder of She Recovers

"We've all had broken hearts. But most of us haven't learned how to heal them. Enter Mal Duane. Mal's Broken Open: Embracing Heartbreak and Betrayal as Gateways to Unconditional Love supports you in the deep work of uncovering old patterns and beliefs so you can heal your shattered heart. As you follow her powerful practices, you will find yourself stepping into wholeness, forgiveness, and self-love–a beautiful foundation for a beautiful future."

JANET CONNER,

best-selling author of *Writing Down Your Soul*

BROKEN

EMBRACING HEARTACHE AND BETRAYAL AS GATEWAYS TO UNCONDITIONAL LOVE

"A delightful life guide full of important information for those of us who want to keep letting go of the painful things that break our hearts. Mal Duane captured my heart with this powerful book! I learned so much that I sucked my highlighters dry!"

MARIA SALOMÃO-SCHMIDT,

best-selling author of *Finally FULL of Yourself: Unlocking Your Spiritual DNA and Oprah Show* guest

"If you have experienced betrayal in your life, then Mal Duane's *Broken Open: Embracing Heartache and Betrayal as Gateways to Unconditional Love* is for you. As Spiritual Life Coach Mal Duane shares her journey from betrayal and devastation to forgiveness, freedom, joy and personal power, you are given the keys to discovering the love for yourself and others that heals your broken heart. A must-read for women who are suffering from betrayal and have become disconnected from their true selves."

MARGARET PAUL, PHD,

best-selling author of *Do I Have To Give Up Me To Be Loved By You?, Healing Your Aloneness, Inner Bonding, Diet for Divine Connection,* and *The Inner Bonding Workbook*

"The shock of a partner's betrayal–whether virtual or occurring in real life–can create a profound collapse of self, a kind of PTSD that can be almost as devastating as living through the trauma of war. But *Broken Open* provides the ultimate roadmap to healing and triumphing over such betrayal, loss, and suffering. It shows how, at our darkest hour, there is the most potential for growth, for the heart to open, for us to move upward and onward to a fulfilling life that is beyond our wildest dreams. Plus, it is so beautifully written and engaging! Definitely give yourself the gift of this book! You will treasure it!"

DR. DIANA KIRSCHNER,

international best-selling author of *Love in 90 Days*

"The heart can be our greatest teacher, for it has wisdom to guide us back to love. This book and Mal's story are a true testament to what it means to live a courageous life with your heart wide open."

SHANNON KAISER,

best-selling author of *The Self-Love Experiment*

"*Broken Open* is the book you need if it is time to rebuild your life and discover a bright future you might not have imagined. Mal Duane, like a great friend, bravely and honestly tells her story, laying out how you can take the steps needed to heal and thrive."

LISA SMITH,

author of *Girl Walks Out of a Bar*

"In her powerful book, *Broken Open,* Mal Duane poignantly reveals how you can heal your wounded heart after being betrayed by someone you love. Through sharing her vulnerable journey of healing, Mal shows you that you have the power to transmute pain into enduring self-love and create a purposeful, happy and love-filled life. A must-read for any woman who desires to transform her broken heart into everlasting love."

DR. DEBRA L. REBLE,

Intuitive Psychologist and international best-selling author

"In her beautifully-written book, Mal offers a path of awareness and healing in finding the gift in a broken heart. Mal's book will surely help people find the path to letting the light back in."

DR. CATHERINE HAYES,

Leadership Coach and international best-selling author of
*Everything Is Going to Be Okay!: From the Projects to
Harvard to Freedom*

"Broken Open is a beautiful book that is a wake-up call for all of us that have been involved with or dependent on unhealthy, untrustworthy people and addictive behaviors. Mal is a powerful force with a unique, fascinating story of deep betrayal and redemption. She learned the hard way how to start over and forgive, and she shows you how to do the same. Mal's story and courage to heal provides a roadmap out of painful choices. Give yourself the gift and read this book, and you will learn how to turn your own pain into power. "

LAURA FENAMORE,

author, speaker, coach and founder of SkinnyFatPerfect.com

BROKEN

EMBRACING HEARTACHE AND BETRAYAL AS GATEWAYS TO UNCONDITIONAL LOVE

"*Broken Open* is a life-changing, must-have resource for anyone aspiring to turn adversity into a pathway to greater self-compassion, healing, and transformation."

LAUREN MACKLER,

best-selling author of *Solemate: Master the Art of Aloneness & Transform Your Life*

"As painful as heartbreak is, it serves a purpose. Betrayal is a call to do things differently. Mal Duane's *Broken Open* takes you through a deep practice to uncover your resilience and emerge as a woman not afraid to stand in her own truth."

SHERRY GABA, LCSW,

author of *The Marriage and Relationship Junkie: Kicking your Obsession*

"Mal Duane is a true inspiration! In this book, she shares clear, powerful steps to healing, strength, and awakening to the new life that's waiting for you. A must-read for anyone who wishes to move beyond heartbreak to find joy again."

KRISTI LING SPENCER,

best-selling author of *Operation Happiness*

"I was drawn right in. With her raw and real personal storytelling of betrayal, Mal Duane brought me right back to my own 'broken open' moment many years back. Too many of us know this experience. Mal empowers you with the words, wisdom, and self-empowerment strategies to understand unhealthy patterns in love and stop being victimized by them. In *Broken Open*, Mal helps you see that you deserve better and shows you how to own it with unconditional self-compassion and self-confidence."

DR. COLLEEN GEORGES,

coach, TEDx Speaker, author of *RESCRIPT the Story You're Telling Yourself*

"I first met Mal as she was emerging from the relationship that broke her open. I have watched her heal from heartache, transforming from coal to a diamond. Her story will inspire anyone who's had a broken heart to learn from the pain, and to use her past as a catalyst for a much better future. Mal is living proof that the cracks are where the light comes in. Read *Broken Open* and find hope and inspiration for what's possible. (Spoiler alert: it's better than you ever imagined!)"

SANDY WEINER,

women's love and empowerment coach, author, and podcast host

"Mal Duane's empowering book, *Broken Open,* is a story of the wounded heart, providing a roadmap back to self - to unconditional love. If you are struggling, this is the book for you. You will laugh, cry, be filled with hope, and move forward consciously choosing healthy relationships that support your best life. This is the movie of your life after all, courageously write your own love story!"

DEBRA OAKLAND,

author of *Change Your Movie, Change Your Life: 7 Reel Concepts for Courageous*

"Life after love is possible! Mal reminds us of the power within ourselves to outlive any heartbreak and come out stronger. Tender and self-loving, *Broken Open* is the handbook for women who are ready to journey back to a place of universal love."

AMY LEIGH MERCREE,

medical intuitive and best-selling author

"Mal holds nothing back with this shocking account of deception and the cathartic healing process after being betrayed by her beloved husband. To paraphrase Broken Open, when you get to the other side of your grief and pain, you will find absolute beauty in what was once broken. Great read!"

XI

SHANN VANDER LEEK,

Transformation Goddess and creator of The Sacred Heart Teachings

BROKEN

EMBRACING HEARTACHE AND BETRAYAL AS GATEWAYS TO UNCONDITIONAL LOVE

"Mal Duane truly understands what it feels like when your heart and your life have broken open; the pain, the heartache and the despair. Her book, Broken Open, is a brilliant, honest, and wise source of guidance and rediscovery through the steps of tender healing as a gateway to of a new, more empowering story of you and a window into unconditional love."

IRIS BENRUBI,

author, speaker, dating and relationship coach

"Broken Open is an empowering book that takes us on a healing journey from broken-heartedness to unconditional love, guiding us to connect with our own wisdom and insight with powerful self-inquiry questions, and other self-nurturing practices like meditation and journaling. Mal nurtures us through this transformative process by sharing her and other women's experiences of being broken open, filling the pages with hope and inspiration!"

KELLEY GRIMES, MSW,

self-nurturing expert and best-selling author

"Oscar Wilde once said, 'To love oneself is the beginning of a lifelong romance.' My friend Mal Duane has passionately expanded on this core truth in her latest book, Broken Open. Right from the start, she welcomes women who are at a point of choice in their emotional lives and lovingly reminds them there is wisdom to be gained from their wound saying, 'We cannot know our divinity and continue to live out the story of our own brokenness.' With each chapter she shares personal insights, failings, fears, and breakthroughs on her life-long journey to let the light of self love penetrate the cracks in her broken heart. Through a series of powerful journaling questions, loving guidance, and a little bit of storytelling sass, Mal becomes the best friend you could ever ask for when going through the fires of hell so you can come out whole on the other side. Let Broken Open be the gift you absolutely must give yourself as you travel the path from powerless to powerful, so you can live and love as a woman of heart."

LINDA BARD,

Intuitive Confidante at Find Your Creative Voice

"Everybody can find strength through these pages because everyone has experienced heartbreak. In Broken Open, Mal invites us into her journey of heartbreak and self love to provide hope for those who are still suffering. Duane leads by example through her bravery and owning her story. The vulnerability in her writing makes her the ultimate warrior and offers a genuine connection for her readers through the power of storytelling."

KELLEY KITLEY, LCSW,

owner of Serendipitous Psychotherapy and best-selling author of MY self: An autobiography of survival

"Heartache is painful and intensely purifying, and yet healing is readily available when we release old stories and powerfully own our part in them. This book blesses with great wisdom as Mal shares her personal experiences and holds your hand to guide you to the sacred space of unconditional love!"

BETH MARSHALL,

Transformational Catalyst and Spiritual Mentor

"Broken Open is heart-engaging and beautifully written. It is a spiritual unfolding of Mal Duane's personal journey of betrayal, grief, and pain to a place of wholeness and ultimate healing. Mal not only describes her own healing from heartbreak, she shares stirring stories of other women she's coached with different love and life experiences. They also needed to find a way to heal their wounds and get to the place of divine love within themselves. The book also has practical and spiritual tools for you, the reader, for breaking free and healing, claiming self-worth, loving yourself, and consciously creating your heart's desire. Not only do you come away feeling healed in some way too, you have a deeper understanding of the qualities of unconditional love so you can experience unconditional love for yourself and in your life."

DR. JO ANNE WHITE,

international award-winning, best-selling author, speaker, producer, Certified Professional Coach, and Energy Master Teacher

FOREWORD

KRISTINE CARLSON

NEW YORK TIMES BEST-SELLING AUTHOR AND
WORLD-RENOWNED SPEAKER

*A*s an inspirational speaker and author, I've stood in countless rooms and asked the question, "Who in this room has not had their heart broken?" I've never had a single person raise their hand. Chances are, if you're opening this book, you have also had your heart shattered into shards, and you're wondering when you will feel more than the pain of loss.

My own life-altering loss came twelve years ago when my beloved husband was traveling by plane to New York from California. He died suddenly and unexpectedly on the descent of the flight from a pulmonary embolism. After the initial shock and an aftermath of pain like I never thought imaginable, a great surprise remained. I was heart-broken open to a deep spiritual awakening and a journey that has revealed so much to me about treasuring life and living my days to the fullest. My loss brought me to the winding road of healing, transformation, and transparent awareness of my true nature. That's the power of love and loss: to awaken you to something more.

Mal has written a poignant and powerful book in *Broken Open*. Her words point us in the direction of healing from heartbreak, and even more so, they steer us toward one of the most powerful human lessons that we are here to experience: what it means to love, to love eternally and unconditionally. It's fascinating that most of us learn this lesson best through the corridor of loss. It is the powerful vehicle that opens the door for us to realize that love itself is always present. Mal shows us that the journey home is about learning to love yourself fully and completely, despite the agonizing way you were forced to get there.

We mustn't compare pain journeys, for not all heartbreak is death. For example, divorce and death represent the same grief that comes from the loss of a dream, the loss of a once-shared hope for a future together. In divorce, you must reconcile the separation as a life-death, and often, sort through the array of complex emotions rooted in a betrayal of commitment or turn away from a cold heart. The former spouse is, after all, not physically absent; the line between what was and what is might feel fuzzy and full of emotional torture. In these ways, there's far more inner reconciliation and work to do after divorce. There might be a higher mountain to climb.

Mal knowingly guides you up that mountain from the richness of her own personal inquiry to the glorious summit, which represents an end and a beginning. My favorite chapter is later in the book, Chapter 11: Freedom is Forgiveness. Mal shows us that clinging to our anger is costly; it's the ultimate act of self-betrayal and keeps us stuck in the past. It is only through the portal of forgiveness that we will subtly shift into a new direction toward a greater expression of love. This inner work will likely be the most difficult task in our pivot out of pain, but Mal takes the reader by the hand and shows us how to do it with grace.

Women are nurturers. Women love easily and readily, but we also give our power away. We are apt to compromise so much that we lose ourselves in the process of loving another. Mal teaches how to reclaim our true nature and never settle for breadcrumbs in a relationship again. Her gentle writing over and over reminds us that we are not the victim. In her own words Mal says, "The men I'd loved hadn't hurt me because I was weak and at their mercy. They'd hurt me because I had given them my power, and made myself powerless in the relationship. They couldn't help but hurt me. I was a doormat waiting to be stepped on." Those sentences give me chills. They paint a picture of a brave woman set free by her own self-awareness and self-love. May we all see our lives with equal clarity and courage, dear friends.

Thank you, Mal, for your vulnerability and candor in sharing your own journey of pain to awakening; it's the healing road that so many long for. By getting stuck in the muck of bitterness and suffering, we miss the greatest part: the joy that inevitably follows. Mal will help so many step through their heartache and toward the true meaning of love. She will show you the beauty that awaits in transformation, as you learn a far better way to engage with love. Mal will teach that the love that comes from the relationship we have with ourselves—self-love—is the most satisfying kind. And she encourages us with the truth that broken hearts mend with time and grace.

One thing I want to highlight for you, my fellow readers, is the journaling process at the back of each chapter. I have found that journaling is one of the most powerful healers there is, and you will discover depths of wisdom that comes from asking yourself the questions Mal has posed. There is no journey greater than discovering who you are on the path of love. And, who you are is worthy and magnificent!

Broken Open holds the keys for you to find what you're looking for, which is so much more than freedom from pain. You will find the power within that comes through the gateway of one of the most painful wounds: a broken heart. As that brokenness mends, your heart will expand and grow to hold even more love and joy than you could have ever imagined. There is so much compassion on the journey, and you are about to step into the sweet embrace of unconditional love that is always present and never abandons.

Treasure the gifts of life and love,

KRISTINE CARLSON

New York Times best-selling author and world-renowned speaker
KristineCarlson.com

Table of CONTENTS

EMBRACING HEARTACHE AND BETRAYAL
AS GATEWAYS TO UNCONDITIONAL LOVE

MAL DUANE

www.inspiredlivingpublishing.com

INTRODUCTION

*W*hen you get knocked down in life, it can leave you breathless, curled up on your knees. Your mind is blurred. Deciphering your next step is almost impossible. I know. I've been there. I have suffered betrayal so profound that I felt like a gutted animal, not knowing if I would survive.

I've also spent the past three years meeting with and interviewing women who have experienced loss, divorce, or betrayal in a relationship. We have so much in common, these women and me. I know their feelings, and their devastation. I know how scary it can be to find yourself suddenly catapulted into a new reality that doesn't look a thing like the old one.

And I also know that the wounds we take in these battles of love are the most profound tools for healing we will ever receive.

So many women I've met have remained caught in their pain after the end of a relationship. Their hearts were broken, and never healed. Months, years, even decades later, they are still living as victims to their past relationships, mired in fear, disconnected from love, filled with poisonous anger and pain that is eating them away from the inside. I tell them, just as I will tell you: this lifelong suffering is a choice. There is a better way.

The pain of betrayal is real. It needs to be felt, and processed. But when you get to the other side of that pain, there is a beauty like you have never seen before. There is healing deeper than any you've previously experienced. And there is a new life full of unconditional love waiting to embrace you.

This book is about being broken open—about having your heart shattered, cracked open to its core. But it's not about the actions that caused your wounds. It's not about rehashing the old story of how you got screwed over, or how badly someone took advantage of you. Instead, this book is a journey of healing and personal transformation. It's about deeply connecting to your feelings, knowing your devastation, and looking within for the answers and love you crave.

The excruciating pain I experienced when my heart was broken open inspired me to look deep inside myself. I examined my old love stories, my patterns, my beliefs about who I was and what I deserved. I asked hard questions, and forced myself to really engage with the answers I received. And, when I embraced my shattered core and brought my deepest fears to light, I found a new version of myself—a woman who can stand in her truth, and whose greatest source of love is her own brilliant heart.

As you work through this book, I ask that you don't judge yourself, your feelings, or your experience. I'll ask you to engage with powerful self-inquiry questions, as well as spiritual practices like meditation and journaling. The more truthful and open you can be with yourself, the greater your capacity for healing will become.

When you do this work, you will stand in the company of other women who have walked through the fires of hell and come out the other side. You will have a new perspective that reflects your authentic self, not a vision controlled by someone else's opinion. You will discover your inner light, and begin to shine it for the world to see.

YOUR JOURNEY BACK TO *Love*

Broken Open is about finding wholeness, forgiveness, and unconditional love for yourself and others after your heart has been wounded by betrayal. I will hold you in a sacred place while you catch your breath and find your footing, so you can follow your path of illumination into the next phase of your life. Remember, your heart may be shattered, but it's still beating. There is still life within you, and it will carry you through this journey.

Your pain may be overwhelming today, perhaps deeper and more profound than any pain you've felt before. Allow yourself to settle into it. Don't resist it, or push it away. While you read the first chapters of this book, let the pain be with you, around you, and beside you. Allowing yourself to feel is one of the most self-loving things you will ever do.

As we move into the process of healing and the exercises I'll assign, remember that you can't change what happened— but you can change the way you relate to it. Your life has been flipped upside down—not to crush you, but to shake loose all of the baggage you no longer need to carry. As you heal old wounds and identify old beliefs that have undermined your choices, you will release outdated patterns that were manipulating you mentally and emotionally, and causing you

3

to make choices that were not in your own best interest. This recognition will initiate a progression of steps to piece together your mind, body, and spirit in harmony, so you can feel and love like a whole woman, maybe for the first time in your life.

The Japanese have a practice called "wabi-sabi," which is about finding beauty in something that appears at first to be ugly and imperfect. Your broken heart isn't a hot, sticky mess of tears and pain; it doesn't need to be a flaw or hideous scar. Instead, it's a badge of courage, an emblem that shows you know how to love deeply.

The crack in your heart has meaning and purpose. It allows a golden light to come through to reveal all that you have been hiding, ignoring, or running from. That light will guide you to release old, negative emotions like fear, judgment, and resentment that have kept you living like a victim. When you see these feelings, honor them, and let them go, you can then replace them with love.

Every single woman I've met who has experienced being broken open has wanted to find some kind of understanding. They ask, "Why did this happen to me?" The work we will do in this book is a pathway to that understanding, and to closure. When you understand the pain you feel, put it in context, and choose a new way forward, you will find a bigger connection to yourself and your own heart than you ever thought possible.

My beautiful sister, we are connected in this lifetime through the experience of being broken open. Today, I am softer than I was before. My heart is scarred, but it is whole. I have more unconditional love for others, for myself, and even for the one who hurt me more than I ever thought possible. I know the real meaning of forgiveness, and I revel in the freedom it has brought me.

It is my profound honor to hold you and help you in your journey to awaken to the new life ahead of you—a life where you can deliberately choose to have more happiness, freedom, and peace of mind, a life where love is endless because it radiates from within you. My wish for you is that you find the healing you desire, so you can come back stronger, wearing your broken heart as a badge of courage.

With great love and compassion,

CHAPTER ONE

THE WOUND AND THE WISDOM

CHAPTER ONE

THE WOUND AND THE WISDOM

"There are two extremes to avoid: being completely absorbed in your pain and being distracted by so many things that you stay far away from the wound you want to heal." - *Henri J.M. Nouwen*

It was the summer of 2013. I was curled up on my knees on the floor. There was a huge lump in my throat, and my heart was pounding so hard that I couldn't get up. Beads of sweat were forming on my forehead. I couldn't speak. I couldn't even think past the one thought that was screaming in my head:

"How could he do this to me?"

A few moments before, I had walked into the home office where my husband of more than ten years spent much of his time. On his computer screen was an image from a video, staring at me. I immediately forgot what I'd come in there for; the screen drew me like a moth to a flame. This was obviously something I wasn't meant to see—and yet, now that I'd seen it, I couldn't *unsee* it. It was like it had branded me, and I was burned through to my core.

I'm not sure how long I stared at that screen with the fears and questions exploding in my mind. My legs were shaking so hard that I couldn't get up. Part of me still couldn't make sense of what I was looking at—and another, deeper part of me was screaming, falling … shattering.

The person I loved and trusted more than any other had broken his vows to me. My future, as I'd been imagining it, had just been obliterated in one explosive moment. And the memories of past heartbreaks, moments on which I thought I'd closed the door forever, were swirling up out of the wreckage, tormenting me as I stood, frozen, in this God-awful moment of revelation.

In that moment, I was broken open.

It took me a good ten minutes to get up. Once I'd gained my feet, I prayed, "Dear God, please show me the way!" Well, there was only one way, even though I didn't want to take it.

Tears streamed down my face as I pulled myself up the stairs to confront him.

He was still sleeping. I knelt at his side of the bed and nudged him because, even though I wanted to scream, I could barely speak. He took one look at me and knew that something was terribly wrong. He reached for my hand, but I pulled away. I couldn't stand him touching me.

"You need to explain something to me," I whispered.

"What's wrong, Mal? What the hell is going on?"

"Come with me. I want to show you something."

I almost lost my balance on the way down the stairs. When we got to the office, I stood in the doorway and pointed at the computer. That awful image was still frozen on the screen.

"Can you please tell me what this is?"

He looked. "Well," he said. "I guess I'm busted."

I almost gagged. "Is that the best you can do? Is that *all you have to say*?"

Apparently, it was.

***

I know you know this feeling. Maybe, like me, you discovered that the love of your life was using "visual aids" to have a sexual experience behind your back. Maybe your Prince Charming ran off with another princess. Maybe your love wasn't enough to save the one you loved from addiction and all of its pitfalls. Maybe the one who was supposed to cherish you above any other caused you greater harm—physically, mentally, and emotionally—than anyone had before. Maybe you discovered that all the promises he made to you were just lies to cover his ass.

The story of how you were broken open is your own, but the feeling is the same for all of us. It's the feeling of being shattered, cracked, laid bare. Suddenly, all of our certainty is swept away. The ground has shifted under our feet, and it has sent us tumbling. We open our eyes to darkness, to an absence of light, and of love. Blinded, we have to feel our way back to safety.

These are the true ramifications of betrayal.

And yet, in all the despair, there is hope. This entire experience can become your greatest learning experience, and your broken heart your greatest teacher—*if* you will allow it.

There are many members in the sisterhood of shattered women, but not all of us make it out of the darkness and back into our light. Some remain stuck in the dark, frozen inside their loss and anger. I don't want that to happen to you—and that's why I'm here to guide you. The path you are about to walk is a hard one, but with a strong hand to hold, you will make it through the valley and see the sun again.

I promise that awakening to the illusions you have created about love, and deeply feeling the pain of being broken open, will serve a higher purpose than you can currently imagine. I had placed my husband on a pedestal—and, like so many other icons, he had fallen. When he did, I felt like my belief in love had been ripped right out of me. However, once I began my transformational work of healing my broken heart, I realized that the true nature of love was only just starting to reveal itself to me.

HOW THE *Light* GETS IN

Right now, you may be asking yourself, "Will I recover? Will I ever be the same again?" The answer is yes … and no. You *will* recover, but you will not be the same. A big piece of you was invested in your relationship; when you reclaim it, it will be different. It will need loving care to heal. But if you do this work—the work I will share with you in this book—you will reemerge into your life more whole, more free, and more full of love than you were before you were broken open.

When your self-worth has been crushed beyond measure by loss or betrayal, it's easy to wonder, "What did I do to deserve this?" The answer is, nothing. You did nothing to deserve this. Betrayal isn't about you, but rather about someone else's behavior and wounds. They are missing a piece of themselves, and they are driven to fill it. You were collateral damage in their internal war—but you didn't cause the war.

I didn't understand that at first. I spent endless hours thinking about how to change my husband's behavior, replaying the movie reels to try to pinpoint the moment when it all went wrong. I promised myself I wouldn't make any rash decisions. I researched his addiction, got us into counseling, and contacted experts around the world. I went to support meetings. I extracted promises. But the more time I spent trying to solve his problems, the deeper he fell into his patterns. I was doing all the work for him, and his behavior wasn't changing one single bit. He would swear to do better only to be caught in a lie a few days later.

And then, one day, I finally realized the truth: I was fucked. There was not one single thing I could do to change him, because he wasn't ready to change.

The last spark of the love I'd once had for him died in me that day. It had been dimmed nearly to extinction by his dishonesty, but the last glimmer of hope lingered for a long, long time. Once I realized that there was no way for us to get back what we had once shared, however, the path was clear. I could stay in my marriage, knowing full well that he would continue to betray me, or I could leave.

I chose to leave. And in leaving, I chose *me*.

To this day, I'm glad I didn't make any quick decisions. I tried every possible option to save our marriage. I gave him every opportunity to be open with me and share what had driven him to that place. And because I was so methodical about every step I took, each decision felt right in my heart. I never doubted my decision to ask for a divorce. After the line was drawn, I never replayed those movies in my head, or asked, "What if?" The time for that was done. My focus was to stay on the high road and do what was right for me, so I could heal and move on with my life.

The road to my healing was challenging sometimes, but with every "a-ha!" moment or piece of resolution I uncovered a new piece of me. I discovered myself as a woman who is filled with love and respect for herself, and prepared to advocate for her needs. I took the single biggest betrayal of my life and turned it into my most amazing gift—the gift that taught me, once and for all, what love truly means, and how I can live it every day.

This early in your process, it can be hard to grasp that there is a higher, divine purpose to the wound you have experienced. Sadly, pain is a necessary teacher for many of us. It gives us the most powerful possible signal that we have been going the wrong way. When we are broken open, it forces us to stop in our tracks, and feel our way back to the path that will lead us to our highest good and expression.

You have been broken open so you can let the light in. You have been cracked so that love can fill you. You have been hurt so you can mend all the shattered pieces of yourself that you never knew were bleeding you dry.

Maybe you never realized until now how many little things you overlooked to keep the peace. Maybe you feel sickened by all the compromises you made that in your heart you knew weren't right. Maybe you loved this other person so much that you lost yourself. Maybe you gave and gave, only to find your own tank empty. Maybe you apologized and changed your behavior when it wasn't your job to do so. These are not isolated incidents. They are pieces of you—subconscious patterns and beliefs that are calling to be healed. The light is shining through the cracks and revealing them for the first time.

You are at a crossroads, sister. From here, you can choose the dark road of bitterness, vengeance, and blame. Or, you can choose the path to light and healing. It's up to you—but before you storm off down that first road, think about this: do you want to wake up five years from now—or ten, or twenty—feeling just as angry and broken as you do today? Or do you want to show up as a woman who loves and advocates for herself, and who embraces her life despite all the hurt she's suffered? Do you want to keep telling everyone how you got screwed over, or do you want to feel unwavering confidence in the woman you are? This is the choice before you.

The healing road isn't always easy, but it's always worth it.

Understanding the nature of heartbreak will teach you more about yourself than you could ever have imagined. It ignites the best and the worst things inside you—and you must be willing to look both of them square in the eyes. Both have significant teaching tools to help you reclaim the piece of yourself that you feel has been ripped away.

Everything has an opposite: yes and no, light and dark, north and south, black and white. When you embrace all of yourself, you embrace not only your strength and magnificence, but your weakness and flaws. You become comfortable with your own imperfections—and, as a result, are less likely to hold deep resentment for and judgment about others. You begin to love your weakness, and stop expecting others to fill you up. The cords that tie you to your painful past are cut, because you realize that the only one holding them in place was you.

FIND THE *Strength* WITHIN

At first, your emotions won't want to let you see the gift in your brokenness. You will need to work through layers of anger and hurt to see the true nature of your wounds. We will do some of that work together as we move through this book, but for now, just begin to be okay with them. You can be angry without blaming. You can be hurt without lashing out. Embrace your feelings, because they will point the way to your healing.

A few days after my awful discovery in my husband's office, I sat quietly and thought about my past relationships. This was not the first time I had been lied to, cheated on, or deeply disappointed. There were still many skeletons in my closet that needed to be cleaned out.

On that day and on many others to follow, I poured my heart onto the pages of my journal. I relived the obsessive need to feel loved that had plagued me since I was a child—a need which had blinded me to others' deceits and made me willing to accept the unacceptable. I held on to relationships that hurt me, over and over again, because I was more afraid of being alone than I was of being treated like shit.

I had done a lot of work over the years to release these patterns. I'd changed constricting beliefs, and stopped my self-sabotaging behaviors. I learned to recognize warning signs. How could this crap still be haunting me? Was I still stuck in some kind of subconscious pattern around my own deservingness of love?

16

"Or," I thought, "Maybe this is all his fault, because he's a no-good bastard."

The more time I spent in introspection, letting my thoughts swirl onto the pages of my journal, the more I realized that something deep within me was calling for healing. And I couldn't access that something when I was projecting everything outward. The more I indulged in my blame, shame, and anger, the less I felt in touch with the truth at my core.

I joined a support group for women who had experienced some form of infidelity. Sometimes I would share, and sometimes, I would just sit quietly and listen to the other women. There was one girl who spoke almost weekly about the ongoing drama of her husband's affairs. Every few days she would find lipstick on his shirt, text messages on his phone, or another woman's belongings in his car. She would sob as she recounted the pain and humiliation of these discoveries, but she didn't have the courage to leave him. She would get so angry that she would pound the table and scream her rage at "that no-good motherfucker."

I had so much empathy for her—but the way she spoke also left me with a huge knot in my stomach. She was so consumed with blaming her husband that she refused to take responsibility for her own well-being. Although she was showing up for support, she wasn't willing to help herself.

As tempting as it was to fall into that behavior, I knew it wasn't going to help me. I wanted to understand at a deeper level what had caused his behavior, and why I hadn't seen this coming. I was trying to wrap my head around the most fucked-up thing that I ever had experienced, and if I let myself fly off the handle, I might never find my way back.

This was one of the most profound lessons for me in my healing: everything ultimately comes from within you. You can't be powerless and powerful at the same time. As long as you see yourself as a victim of your partner's behavior, you will never find the power to heal yourself.

Your responsibility right now is to get back up. Pick yourself up off the floor and stand tall. It doesn't matter if your knees are shaking, and your voice is choked with tears. It doesn't matter if you feel stripped naked. Get up. No one else can do this for you. You can reach out for support, but it's not someone else's responsibility to bear your weight. Instead, reach for the strength within you. It's there, and it always has been.

YOUR DAILY *Divine* GUIDANCE

In every chapter of this book, I'll share questions, exercises, and techniques to help you experience a new level of healing and awareness. Many of them will take you deep into the pain you're feeling, but don't put them off. Start to pull back all the layers that you have created over the years to hide the authentic, marvelous you. The more you can love yourself through the pain, the quicker and more miraculous your healing will be.

Today, and every day from now on, I want you to write in your journal. If possible, do this first thing in the morning. There are no rules for this writing except one: don't ever put a lie on this paper. This is your sacred space for healing. Here, you can be fully honest with yourself.

Light a candle. Take a few deep breaths. Then, pour your heart onto those pages. Let all the hurt and pain and questions come up. Don't judge anything that comes out, just let it flow. Then, when you feel emptied out, write out this question:

"What can I do today to help myself?"

Sit with this question, and allow whatever comes up. Write down anything that flashes in your mind. Divine guidance is fast. If you question and doubt it, it will disappear. Above all, listen to your heart. Although she has been wounded, she will talk to you. Ask her for clarity and strength. She wants to nurture you and see you whole again.

This one question will change your whole day. You'll be focused on what you can do, instead of what went wrong. As you go about your day, follow the guidance you received. Then, before you go to bed at night, go back and reread what you wrote that morning. What stands out to you? What wisdom did you gain?

The more you practice this, the more detached from your anger and resentment you will become. You can let those feelings live on the pages, instead of in your heart. After a while, you may feel your mind step out of the way, and make room for messages from a higher power, or a more enlightened version of you.

One very powerful message I received in my journaling process told me "I could assume anything but still know nothing. Stick to what I know for sure. Stick to the facts and the right decisions will be made." Holy crap. That blew my mind. I hadn't realized how much I was assuming and projecting until that moment.

If you already have a journaling practice, you can do this work in the way that feels best for you. If you don't, consider the questions below as prompts for your daily writing. And if you don't have a journal, now is the perfect time to get one.

SELF-REALIZATION QUESTIONS

- Do you feel responsible in any way for your partner's behavior? Why?

- Does anything feel familiar in this situation? Have you experienced this kind of betrayal or situation before?

- What positive thing have you learned about yourself since the moment you were broken open?

- What "a-ha" moments have you had while reading this chapter?

***

The light coming through the crack in your heart is illuminating a new path for you. It has the power to burn away the old distortions of yourself and create a powerful inner transformation of freedom.

This work starts with letting go of blame and recognizing both your wound and the wisdom that lies within it. You don't need to know what you will learn, or how you will grow, only that you will learn, and you will grow.

If you make this journey with me through the pages of this book, you will learn to stand strong again in who you are. From this place of vulnerability, you will find your strength. In this darkness, you will learn to cherish the light. From this pain, you will come to understand love with a new respect and fervor. From this place of being broken open, you will experience true healing from within.

CHAPTER TWO

YOUR LOVE STORY

CHAPTER TWO

YOUR LOVE STORY

"Real self-love is the hard kind—the kind that requires
the courage to be honest with yourself, to have the hard
conversations, and to make the tough decisions you
know you need to make." - *Mel Robbins*

*L*ove is your true nature. It's how you arrived here on Earth at
birth—a perfect, divine little being, a clean slate untouched by
opinions or perceptions. Then, you met your parents ... and a
new story began.

As children, we quickly forget the truth of divine love and
instead take on human narratives about love. We watch how
our parents love one another, and how they withhold love. We
learn that we need to look, or act, or be a certain way in order
to be loved. We learn that some people are "lovable," while
others are not.

Most of all, we learn that when we aren't "good," don't fit
in, or don't act according to others' expectations, love can be
taken away.

These stories become our image of love. When something
doesn't conform to that image, we become threatened and

consumed by fear. We might withhold love when what's happening doesn't fit our definitions. Or, we might try to manipulate the person we love into acting or feeling in a way that lines up with our definitions of what love should be.

Everything we do from a place of fear pushes love further away. When we can't hold onto the love we want, we become full of resentment and anger. Our suffering increases. We are desperate to fill the void that fear has left within us, but our solutions aren't working. And so we turn to even more destructive behaviors, hoping that if we can't have love, at least we don't have to feel the pain.

My wounds began in childhood. Starting in my mid-teens, I felt completely unlovable. I was taller than all of my friends, thin as a rail, and looked completely different from all of my siblings. My ears stuck out. I felt like a freak. All I wanted to do was hide.

When I ventured into modeling at the age of twenty, my height and weight became assets. Being five-foot-eleven and 103 pounds was a requirement, not a deficit—but the sudden 180-degree shift in others' perceptions of me didn't heal my wounds, or my fear of being unlovable. Having a portfolio full of extraordinary pictures taken for magazines and billboards didn't convince me of my worthiness. People would rave about the beautiful young woman in my photo, but I didn't *feel* beautiful. I felt like the same old Mal with the big ears, slouching her way through the corridors of her high school with a headband covering her giant ears.

And so, I did the fashionable thing: I drank.

My Band-Aid was a pitcher of stingers, brandy, and crème de menthe. Alcohol numbed the pain and helped me forget, if only temporarily, how worthless I really felt. Some women comfort themselves with food; others use sex, work, or shopping. And hey, if those don't work, there's always isolation. I tried them all—but each of them only became an excuse to drink more.

As they say, you pick your poison.

But the poison isn't really what's hurting us. Our addictions are symptoms, not causes. The poison—whether it's work, sex, flirtation, sleep, shopping, drinking, drugs, or something else entirely—is actually what we perceive as the remedy. And we keep trying to douse ourselves with it over and over, never realizing that it's our story about love—and our deservingness of love—that's causing our pain.

The first big love of my life (I'll call him Mitch) was drawn to me because of my modeling. He liked me for my looks—and I became addicted to his attention. I followed him around like a puppy. I drove into the city each night to see him because he worked late in his business. When he was laid up with a back injury, I drove an hour each way to minister to him nightly. I was dependent on him to make me feel worthwhile. And for a little while, it worked. Somebody loved me. The world was all right.

Almost a year into the relationship, I went away for a week. It was the first thing I had done on my own since we started dating. When I got home, I could feel the difference in Mitch the moment I walked through the door.

"What's wrong?" I asked, with tears in my eyes. "Did something change while I was gone?"

"I just don't want to be tied down," he snapped.

He wanted to be free to do as he pleased, he said—but I knew in my heart that he had already started doing just that. I slunk out of his house like a kicked dog … and went straight to my poison for comfort.

Because of the unhealthy dependency I had on Mitch, it took

a very long time for me to heal. My connection to him defined who I thought I was. For several years, I pined away for what we'd had, while my drinking increased exponentially. I tried to turn every new man I met into a carbon copy of Mitch—which ultimately created one disaster after another. Every time another relationship would implode, I would slip further and further into my black hole.

I know, I know. It's a depressing story. But here's the thing: all of those times, in all of those relationships, I wasn't really in love. I was in my *story* of love, and my choices recreated that story in my life over and over again. It was like reading the script from a single act of a single play, over and over and over again, expecting the lead character's lines to change mid-scene.

WHAT'S YOUR *Story?*

The path to healing your broken heart begins with your love story.

No, I'm not talking about the fairy tale you keep telling yourself you'll have someday (or, worse, the one you're telling yourself you'll never have). I'm talking about your inner story about love—the one you learned when you were young, and the one you've been acting out in your relationships in one way or another ever since.

We all know that love is extremely powerful. It's taken down empires, started wars, and caused suicides. It's mesmerizing, a magnet, and a powerful tool for manipulation. It can literally create miracles. When we are in love, we feel unstoppable. We have a false sense of being able to do anything. It's like a drug, and it has the same overwhelming effects.

But love—real, true, divine love—isn't an adrenaline rush. It doesn't deny, and it doesn't wear off. It only embraces, and heals. Real love will never start a war, no matter how beautiful the maiden in need of rescue. Real love will never drive someone to despair, or use their feelings against them. Real love will show you the best version of yourself, and expect you to live into it.

The dividing line between real love and the love we act out in our lives is our *story*.

And what creates our love story? You guessed it: *fear*.

(Fear doesn't come from your heart; it's something you create mentally.) I had a story that I needed a man to love me, because alone, I felt unlovable. When Mitch loved me, I felt whole. When he left, the glue that had been holding me together cracked and crumbled.

(The elation and the pain of love are the roller coaster we live on when we are loving from an unhealed place)(The upswing happens when the other person is playing their role according to the expected script—our idea of what love "should" look and feel like.) For my younger self, it was a man saying all the right things, telling me I was beautiful, buying me flowers, "showing me off" to his friends, and acting like he valued me. The downward plunge begins when those expectations are unfulfilled—when the object of our love starts doing, saying, or being things that don't line up with our love story, and therefore makes us feel unloved, confused, or out of place. This is when things start to get crazy.

(When our love story goes off the rails, we might try to recreate love through manipulation.) We might try to become someone different, to fit more easily into our partner's love story. Or we might withdraw, fearing that another high might simply be the precursor to another downward spiral. None of these things are the answer, because none of these things move us toward healing that original wound, which of course is the story itself.

What makes love unique is that it is more than an emotion. It's a divine energy—*the* divine energy. Love never changes; only our perception of it does. Love is eternal, and all-encompassing. It doesn't come from outside of us; it radiates from within us.

Love is the foundation of everything, and it's natural that we, as humans, should want to feel it. We are wired for love and loving connection. But our first experience of love is often of receiving it from others—our parents and caretakers—and so we expect all love to come to us from outside of ourselves. When we shift our story to allow for love to come from within, everything changes.

I worked with a young woman named Alicia who deeply believed that the only way she could "get" love was to do exactly what her boyfriend wanted. Whatever he asked for, she agreed to. Before long, he was asking her to do things that went against her religious beliefs and upbringing. He manipulated her into engaging in sexual acts that made her deeply uncomfortable—including threesomes, which made her feel physically ill.

After every encounter, she felt more and more horrible about herself. But what would happen if she didn't go along with what he wanted? Would he stop loving her? Would he leave her? She was so traumatized that she started pulling her hair out in patches. She couldn't sleep or eat. When she looked in the mirror, she felt nothing but disgust and condemnation.

After several weeks of working with me, Alicia felt ready to confront her boyfriend and tell him that she would no longer participate in the demeaning behavior. As expected, he pushed back, but this time she didn't capitulate. She still had some trouble letting go, but she was able to stop pulling her hair out, and she started sleeping better at night.

It took another few months for Alicia to realize that she wasn't a horrible, faithless sinner because of the things she had done. She was simply desperate to feel loved. What her boyfriend had been demanding of her was not love. It was only her story about love that led her to believe that she needed to compromise her values to get and keep love.

Maybe you've also played that game of compromise. I know I have. And each and every time I set aside my values to give someone else what they wanted, I got a huge pit in my stomach. "Holy shit," I'd think. "That really wasn't worth it." And yet, I made those kinds of compromises again and again, right up until my last marriage.

Often, it's not until we are broken open that we realize that our love story is a sham. Suddenly, we have nothing to hold onto, no more script to follow. At that point, we have two choices. We can heal our love story and embrace unconditional love from within, or we can sink into fear.

When you react from fear, it motivates you to make choices that ultimately hurt you more, and write an even more incorrect story about love and your deservingness of it. More, it can create a mindset of retaliation. When you start striking out at the one who shattered your love story, you deplete your own valuable energy. You do things that aren't in alignment with who you are. It's natural to want to hurt the person who hurt you, but acting on that impulse will only end up making things worse for you.

My client Marie became really vindictive against her old boyfriend. She would do anything to disrupt his life. She even went so far as to spread lies about him to anyone who would listen. As you might expect, this backfired spectacularly. People started referring to her as "a woman scorned," like she was some artifact of another era. She became consumed with anger and bitterness.

29

It became obvious that she had a problem when even her friends started to pull away. They simply couldn't be around her negativity any longer. This was the rude awakening Marie needed to choose a new path and a new love story for herself.

If you choose a feeling of love over a feeling of hatred or bitterness, even just for a moment, you will create a path of clarity which will ultimately cast a powerful light into the break in your heart. Love is powerful energy. It illuminates, and it heals whatever it touches. When your mind isn't clouded by revenge, anger, or spite, you will be able to see yourself more clearly, and make new choices about your future.

REWRITING *the* SCRIPT

If you look back across your life, you will probably notice that certain elements of your love story replay themselves over and over again. These will almost always be directly tied to your deep wounds around love and your worthiness to be loved.

This is by divine design. Your concept of love is a mirror, a reflection of the beliefs you hold about yourself. These beliefs are the script for your play; they create your outcomes and your attachments. And your relationships will keep breaking you open along the same fault lines until you open wide enough to let the light in and heal them.

You have not chosen the things that have happened to you. The behavior of those who broke you open is not your responsibility. However, you *are* responsible for the beliefs about love, and about yourself, that make these types of behavior possible, permissible, and even acceptable in your world. It's a painful reality that your concept of your own worthiness and lovability attracts like behavior from others. If you are putting energetic vibrations out that you are not deserving, or that you don't value yourself, others will match that paradigm. Accepting responsibility for the things you believe about love and yourself opens you to looking at love in new ways and helps you establish better boundaries—as my client Alicia was able to do with her boyfriend.

It's very important at this time not to let yourself slip into victim energy. You are not a victim. You have simply been operating under a false premise: that you need love to be whole, and that you have to look, think, act, or be a certain way in order to "get" it. Now that you know the difference between real love and your love story, you have the power to change what isn't working, and invite in a new experience of love—love *for* yourself, from within yourself.

Because love is a mirror, all relationships are a form of projection. We can use the behavior of others in our lives to see what about us needs to be healed.

One of the most common behaviors I see in my clients' lives is that of "the silent treatment." Maybe you've both silently agreed not to discuss a problem. Maybe you're not confident enough to speak about what's troubling you, or you're afraid if your significant other saw your vulnerability he would leave you. Maybe you keep saying "I'm fine!" when you really want to blow a gasket. Any way you look at it, the silent treatment is feeding into your story about love—about what it looks like, who deserves it, and what makes it leave.

The silent treatment is a simple example of this. It gets far more painful and convoluted with deep betrayal, but the core concepts are the same. We're tempted to rationalize it, to look for all the ways we may have caused it. We would rather pretend that we messed up our lines than admit that our whole script is incorrect.

When I first found out about my husband's betrayal, I tried to put it all on me. My faulty love story told me that I had failed in some way. I thought I had left that gangly, unlovable girl behind years before—but when I was broken open, she was still standing right there, desperate for love while at the same time believing she didn't deserve it.

"Could I have done better?" I wondered. "Could I have prevented this?"

The answer was a definitive "*Fuck*, no!" There was nothing I had done or hadn't done that warranted these kinds of actions. This was deep, dark, deceitful, and well-calculated … and it had nothing to do with me. I was not going to accept responsibility for his bad behavior.

My part in my husband's betrayal was simply this: My story about love, and who I was in love, led me to ignore what should have been obvious signs. I had repeatedly suppressed my intuition because I had allowed my ideals of love and my story of my relationship with my husband to become more important than the truth inside me.

The more deeply I looked into myself, the more I saw how much a part of my love story betrayal had become. What I learned through journaling and introspection was that I am a deeply honest, committed woman whose foundation in life is truthfulness. I wasn't always aware of how important truth was to me, or how often I pushed my need for truthfulness aside in relationships. But now that I had seen it, I couldn't unsee it.

I realized that, even as a mature woman, I was still naïve, even childlike, about trusting people—especially men. I believed what they told me. I believed that they would be honest with me. I mean, why would they lie? If I did feel uncomfortable, or question their truthfulness, I would chalk it up to being insecure. I'd say, "That's your lack of self-esteem again, Mal," when in fact my body and intuition were screaming at me to "look out!"

A perfect example of this happened a few months and many dates into my relationship with my husband. We had discussed being in a monogamous relationship. We had not been intimate yet; I was nursing a broken arm, and still leery of getting into a new relationship until I had confirmation that it was the right one for me.

On Friday night, I prepared a wonderful dinner of lobster bisque, swordfish, and Caesar salad. We listened to beautiful music, and talked about what was next for both of us. He mentioned that he had a commitment the next night; a friend was flying in to see her daughter at college, and he'd agreed to meet her for dinner.

"I'll call you on Sunday, though," he said.

The call never came.

Deep in my core, I knew something was up. My stomach was in knots, but I decided not to do anything. I'd wait it out, and see what he had to say for himself.

I finally got a call late Monday afternoon. He sounded cheerful, like nothing was wrong. I hesitated, but the question was burning a hole in my chest. "Why didn't you call me on Sunday?" I blurted. "You told me you would."

"I just lost track of time," he said, nonchalantly. "Sorry."

My heart was pounding. This wasn't right. I wanted to scream, "*I don't believe you! You're lying to me!*" But all I said was, "It's okay. Don't worry about it."

The lie twisted in my gut like a snake. "Are you crazy?" my mind asked. "You don't want to blow this relationship over your paranoia!" But I swallowed the words, and my pride, in one painful gulp, and moved on with the conversation. The following weekend, we slept together for the first time.

Years later, during our divorce proceedings, it came out that he had, in fact, slept with that woman. And he'd come to me the following weekend as though nothing had happened. The deepest wound—the one I first felt decades before with Mitch's betrayal—had happened to me again. And it happened not because my husband lied to me (although he had), but because I had ignored my intuition in order to keep from looking clingy and insecure.

(His actions weren't my fault ... but this betrayal? I'd allowed this to happen. My story of how our love "should" be had become more important than my greatest value, truthfulness.]

(All my life, I had put men on pedestals) even—or maybe especially—the ones who had no business being there. I was lousy at dating. I never felt on equal ground. I was always overcompensating to make things work, and I got breadcrumbs in return. My blatant neediness pushed any healthy relationships away, which just made me feel more desperate. I think, in some cases, my clinginess actually created, or at least fed, their dishonesty.

I'd thought I was past all that. Twenty-plus years of sobriety and personal growth work had helped me to shed the constant pain and longing. But obviously, that crack in myself hadn't grown wide enough to truly let love in, because here I was again, making the same horrible mistake.

At the same time, there was something empowering about the fact that some part of me had known what was happening. I wasn't powerless. I just needed to become a better listener.)

The more digging I did, the more I discovered that, more

often than not, my intuition had been right. I had just allowed my mind to squash it because it didn't fit with the story I was telling myself about love and relationships. The pain of this betrayal was God-awful, but accepting that I had a part in creating it actually felt empowering. It meant that I wasn't at the mercy of men, or some terrible fate. I could choose something new for myself. I could let the light in, and see what needed to be seen.

My consistent journaling practice during this time helped me unravel my faulty stories about love, and connect to the truth deep within my soul. Every day, I would meditate for about thirty minutes, asking, "What is true for me, and what am I simply assuming to be true? Where do I need to look deeper?" Then, I would write, and let the answers pour out of me. Each day, I would get another piece of the bigger picture, and take another step toward wholeness.

My soul knows love. My soul is *made* of love, because it's part of the divine. And as long as I listen, my soul will never steer me wrong.

The same is true for you. You can rewrite your old love story. You can own your part in allowing what has happened to you, and learn from it. Getting clear about what the crack in your heart is revealing is the first step.

I won't lie—it's easier to avoid this inner work than to dive into it, especially when your wounds are fresh. But the sooner you surrender to the truth that is buried deep within you, the sooner you will come back from the brink.

You can begin by looking at where your intuition and your story about love didn't line up. Here are some questions for your journaling practice to help you dive deeper.

SELF-REALIZATION QUESTIONS

- What is your story about love? How has it shown up in your life? Where did it begin?

- What is the common thread in all of your past relationships? What does this tell you about your love story?

- Do you feel that you deserve unconditional love? Why or why not?

- When have you ignored your intuition or stopped yourself from expressing your feelings? What did this lead to?

- Where have you tolerated inappropriate behavior, dishonesty, or emotional unavailability from your partner?

- Where have you made being in a relationship more important than the quality and lovingness of that relationship?

- How can you show up for yourself with greater love in this moment?

You are on a journey of self-discovery. By looking deeply into the crack in your heart, however painful the process might be right now, you are inviting more love into your life. You will start to identify the old patterns of love relationships that have led you to hurt and despair, and instead open yourself to a new, empowering experience of love from within.

It's okay to grieve what you've lost. It's okay to have moments of rage, or denial, or heart-wrenching sorrow. These are a natural part of the grieving process. But don't let these moments write your story about who you are, or what you deserve in love. Instead, let them point you to the parts of your story that need to be erased forever.

My understanding of the betrayal I experienced in my marriage has changed me dramatically. For the first time, I got a clear and complete look at my personal love story, and how it was, quite literally, fucking up my life. I was able to stare down the dark side of my pain until I could see the light of my own resurrection. I was no longer a woman who had been crucified by betrayal, but a woman who had been given an unprecedented opportunity to heal a repetitive path of betrayal in her life. I would no longer choose to "purchase" love at the cost of my self-worth. I could scrap my story about being a poster child for screwed-up relationships, and instead become a beacon of real, divine love.

When we love ourselves, we know true love, because we recognize the light of the divine within us. We cannot know our divinity and hate ourselves at the same time. We cannot know our divinity and compromise our intuition and integrity. We cannot know our divinity and continue to live out the story of our own brokenness.

You have so much wisdom within you, sister. You have the power to do exactly what I did. You can accept that this pain has a purpose. You can revive your intuition, your self-worth, and your lovability. You can do your inner work, forgive the ones who have hurt you, and forgive yourself for living out a story that created pain. You can tear down the walls around your heart, and start building something new: an unshakable foundation of love for your future.

From here, girl, the only way to go is up.

CHAPTER THREE

WHO YOU REALLY ARE

CHAPTER THREE

WHO YOU REALLY ARE

"Your worst enemy cannot harm you as much as your own unguarded thoughts." - Buddha

I was ten years old the first time someone called me "Dumbo." I got it—my ears stuck out. *Way* out. I looked like the baby elephant in the Disney movie. Ha, ha. But being called "Dumbo" did more than just make me cringe every time I looked in the mirror. It reinforced for me that not only was I ugly, I was also dumb.

That nickname branded my child's heart. I let it in, and treated it as true. Soon, I started asking my parents to have my ears fixed so I didn't have to be Dumbo anymore. This was a complicated procedure in which they would pin my ears to my scalp with stitches. Of course, my parents said "Absolutely not!" With my initial plan shattered, I started wearing headbands over my ears to flatten them out.

Now, I understand that it wasn't the words that wounded

me; it was the story I created around them. I let someone else's offhand teasing dictate my ideas about who I was. And from the moment I accepted "Dumbo" as my self-identity, all the words others spoke about my beauty, intelligence, and worth were cut out of my self-narrative. I heard them as whispers, while "Dumbo" was a scream.

It took me many years of therapy, sobriety, and deep introspection to release the pain I'd taken on when I became Dumbo. Now, I know myself as a beautiful, empowered, authentic woman. I don't give a shit about what my ears look like, because they aren't part of my story about myself any longer.

THE REAL STORY OF *You*

In Chapter Two, we looked at your love story and how it has shaped your relationships. We looked at how the script you were following may have led straight to the moment where you were broken open—and we also looked at how you can begin to rewrite your love story so it has a happy ending.

But here's the thing: *You* are the lead character in your love story. This story is yours; it's about you, and it flows around you. If you want to write a radically different love story, you need to change out of the costume you've been wearing— meaning, the labels you've internalized about who you are and what you deserve in your life—and start showing up as who you truly are.

And who you truly are is *divine*.

Your parents may have consummated a physical act, but your blueprint existed in the cosmos long before you came to this earth. Your soul was *waiting* to be birthed. You chose the timing, the souls who would parent you, your gender expression, and even some of your life's details, all before you drew your first breath. You had a plan for how you would evolve, what you intended to experience, and the lessons—both blissful and challenging—that you would live out in your human body. You chose your path based on what you wanted to learn, and what you needed to heal from past lifetimes.

Yes, on some level, you *chose* this.

I want to be super-clear about this concept, because it's easy to turn this revelation into a source of shame or guilt, or turn it around to try to take responsibility for your partner's actions. That's not what this is about at all.

You didn't choose to be broken open. You didn't choose what your partner did. You did not choose to be betrayed, abused, or left behind, and you don't "deserve" the hurt you are feeling right now. What happened is not your fault.

(But you *did* choose the lesson that being broken open is trying to teach you.) You came to this planet, in part, to learn the wisdom that this experience can give. You acted out your old love story up to this juncture, because it was part of your learning.)

If you choose not to learn the lesson now, you'll be given another opportunity in another way—and another, and another.

I had dozens of opportunities in my life to learn the lessons chosen by my soul. I wasn't ready to learn them. And so I kept acting out the same shitty love story over and over again, until I was finally cracked so deeply, and my heart broken open so wide, that I could let the light in and change my love story for good.

When you look at your current experience of being broken

open, do you recognize an aspect that has happened before in another relationship? If you look closely, chances are that you will. My common denominator was that, in every relationship, I trusted the man more than my intuition. My body was sending up red flares and delivering gut punches to my navel area, but I ignored the warnings. Trusting myself didn't fit with my story about who I was; "Dumbo" didn't know any better than to go where she was led. But each time I ignored the warnings, there was a painful outcome in my love story.

Our lives are comprised of patterns. These patterns are made of behaviors, expectations, and actions—but mostly, they're made of stories. Our stories lead us to our lessons. And only when we learn those lessons can we change the neural pathways which dictate our thoughts, our beliefs, and eventually our outcomes.

Again, it all comes down to choice. Just as we chose this life for ourselves before we even came here, we can choose to live differently while we're here. We can choose new thoughts to think, new stories to tell about ourselves, and new scripts to follow in our relationships. We can write a new story about who we are, and why we're here, at any time. That's part of the power we were given when we chose to have this experience as a divine being in a human body.

THE ROLE YOU'RE *Playing*

Before we can write a new starring role for ourselves in our life story, we need to understand our current story and how it came to be. This isn't so that we can wallow in past (or current) dramas, but so we can clearly see what our current story is trying to tell us about the lessons we came here to learn.

This is, as they say, the "elephant in the room."

For me, it was literally an elephant, thanks to my "Dumbo" nickname. For you, it's probably something else—but if you look at the words that have stuck to you from childhood, and the judgments about yourself that those words created, you will be on track to finding the common thread.

Can you remember the first painful impression you experienced? What judgment did you made about yourself as a result of it? *that I could not be loved for who I was.*

My dear friend Mary was a very enthusiastic child who was told over and over again that she was too loud. Friends and family would ask, "Do you *have* to talk so much? Why can't you just be quiet?" After years of hearing words like those, she began to change. She became withdrawn. She felt that the only way she could be loved was to be quiet. And so she bit her tongue when she wanted to talk. She ate everything on her plate when she wasn't hungry. And she never stood up for herself, even when she knew she should.

As an adult, she put up with a lot of abuse because she believed that speaking up for herself would cause people not to love her. People walked all over her because they knew she wouldn't say no. It all came to a head when she finally found the courage to leave the husband who was abusing her.

"He was attracted to the fake me," Mary told me. "The me who had nothing to say—the quiet me who did what she was told. That should have been a warning right from the start. When he started hitting me, I wanted to scream at him that it wasn't right for him to hurt me. But being hurt wasn't as scary as him not loving me anymore."

Our stories about who we are create roles for us to play.

When we step into those roles, we attract the people who will help us live them, and learn the lessons they have to offer. We think that being someone else will make us more lovable, but the truth is that the more layers of story we add, the more we conceal who we *truly* are—the true, divine beauty within us.

My Dumbo theme was only the first of many layers of story I carried about my lack of worth. The second layer was added when I was in my teens. Someone called me flat-chested. Well, you can imagine how I ran with that one. I wore padded bras until I was eighteen, when I finally developed, trying to fake a level of beauty and confidence I couldn't feel inside.

The story kept hounding me, day in and day out. I was too tall. I was too skinny. I had no boobs. My incessant thinking magnified the differences so that they became intolerable. I couldn't look in the mirror, because when I did, I saw a freakish young woman who was utterly unlovable. I was flawed inside and out.

The worst part was, I truly believed that there was nothing I could do about any of it. I believed that I had to live with this pain forever.

The only way I knew how to deal with this pain was to drink. When I drank, I felt accepted, even loved. I could set aside my self-loathing and just be for a little while.

It wasn't until I got to recovery that I was able to see that it wasn't *who I was* that had caused all of my suffering. It was *my thoughts about myself.* My thoughts—the stories I had been telling myself about myself—were the root cause of my problem, and the reason I kept living out the same painful love story with man after man.

You are not the negative thoughts you have about yourself.

You are not the ugly misfit you think you are. And you are not unworthy because your relationship status has changed, or you suffered a loss. You are not less of a woman because you have been broken open. You are a divine feminine creature who is finally privileged—yes, *privileged*—to get a good look at the fucked-up stories you've been telling yourself about yourself, and finally do something to fix them.

You didn't ask to live through this. You didn't choose to be betrayed, abused, or left behind. But on some level, you did attract these experiences, because the story you told yourself about yourself allowed them to happen.

Maybe, like me, your story led you to ignore your intuitive knowing that he was up to no good. Maybe your story, like Mary's, allowed you to believe that you had to stay silent to be lovable. Maybe your story actually allowed for it to be okay for him to treat you like shit, because "that's what men do."

Again, you didn't "ask for" what happened to you. You didn't choose it, at least not consciously. And it's *not okay* that someone abused or took advantage of you.

What I *do* want you to accept is that you had choices, and you made them. I chose to ignore my husband's odd behavior, and tell myself that I was just being insecure, because my insecurity was part of my story. Now that I have rewritten my story, I have empowered myself to show up as a woman whose intuition is always on point, and who always listens to her inner knowing. I am a woman who loves herself as a divine being deserves to be loved, and I expect others to love me that way, too.

What a difference a new story makes!

WRITING YOUR *New* STORY

By understanding your power to choose the story you tell yourself, you can start to create a new reality. The crack in your heart can be fixed only by you, and by your new choices. No one else can soothe the wounds within you. The light coming through the crack in your heart is trying to show you where your old story has led you into suffering. It's revealing the unconscious choices and repetitive patterns buried beneath your conscious thoughts.

Love is your true essence. You didn't just come here to learn painful lessons; you came here to learn to give and receive love unconditionally, even in challenging conditions. When your heart gets broken, it's natural to shut down to protect your heart and pull your love back. But don't start telling yourself stories about how you need to be harder and less vulnerable to protect yourself, because that will only lead you deeper into your old story. Instead, be proud of yourself for the willingness you have shown to lean into love, to make a commitment, and to be vulnerable with your feelings. You were broken open because you loved. That love might have been less than perfect, but it was a start—a step in the right direction.

Right now, you're in a precarious place. The stories you tell yourself about love when you are still broken open can lead you into the light, or deeper into the dark.

Like we talked about in Chapter One, you are at a point of choice. You can blame love for your current pain, and create a story about how love is nothing but hurt. You can let your fear of being alone, of being hurt again, take hold of your thoughts, and start showing up in your story as a bitter, spiteful character who mistrusts love and everything it touches. (And, let me tell you, if you let yourself step into that story, no hero is going to save you from it.) Or, you can let the light in, and ask, "Where does my story need to change? What do I need to know? What can I learn about myself here?" Instead of running from your uncomfortable feelings, let them in. Sit with them. When you do this, you will uncover powerful seeds of self-realization.

Your journaling practice for this chapter is to sit with your current feelings in a loving way, and listen to what they have to tell you. How are they feeding your old stories about who you are and what you need to do to be loved?

Depending on any kind of external remedy will never bring you the clarity and courage you need to reclaim your life from the hot mess that broke you open. You have to be willing to look within, and go right to the source. Buddhists have a great practice that directs: "Embrace your anger to calm it, then look deeply into it." When you run from pain or anger, you drag it with you. If you sit quietly, allow it, feel it, even journal about it, you weaken the hold it has on you. The more aware you are of what is going on inside your head and heart, the more capable you are of discerning what you need to regain emotional balance. Your pain can create a powerful self-nurturing practice moving forward if you are willing to lean into it.

Trust yourself now. Get quiet, and allow your truth to surface. Pour it out onto the pages of your journal. The answers you need to heal your heart are there. Just give them a chance to emerge.

SELF-REALIZATION QUESTIONS

Work with these questions every day for at least two weeks. You can do this as a single practice, or combine it with the other journaling practices in this book. This is what I call an "emotional barometer," and it will help you understand the ebb and flow of your emotions and how they impact the way you receive and interact with love in your life.

- What are your predominant feelings right now? Identify the top three emotions.

- Now, ask yourself, "What is the main trigger for each of these feelings?"

- Ask, "Have I experienced these feelings before? In what situation?"

- "Am I blaming myself or my partner for these feelings?"

- "What steps can I take today to shift these feelings and the stories I'm telling myself about them?"

You can support your journaling activities with good books on personal growth. (I've included a list of my favorites in the back of this book.)

Many of the women I have worked with have grown immeasurably from this kind of journaling practice after they were broken open. Their burning desire to feel better and get their lives back inspired them to do the internal work needed to heal their old stories and write better ones. It's not a fast fix, but it is the foundation for a lifelong commitment to your well-being.

To help you see what this kind of self-inquiry can reveal, I'll share some seeds of wisdom that came to my clients while they were engaged in this practice of looking at their feelings every day without judgment or attachment. The words of wisdom which came through them gave their broken hearts a whole new meaning and context.

- "I had a greater capacity for love than my partner did."
- "I chose not to change myself to meet my partner's needs in this capacity."
- "My partner was unable to meet my needs in this capacity."
- "I sacrificed my emotional boundaries to keep the peace."
- "I was holding onto my insecurities."
- "I should feel heartbroken, but in a way I'm happy to be free."

WHOSE *Story* IS THIS, ANYWAY?

It's important, as you look at your own stories about who you are and what love means, to remember that your partner—the one who broke your heart open—also lives by stories about love and lovability. That doesn't make what they did right, or acceptable, but it can give context to their actions. For whatever reason, they were unable to love you unconditionally. They were struggling with their own issues. And even though you tried, you couldn't change their story for them—just as no one can change your story but you.

I remember thinking that there was a deep current of dissatisfaction coming from my husband at various points in our marriage. It was like he would give off energetic waves periodically. He would appear consumed by something on television so as not to have to interact with me. I felt he didn't see or hear me—which of course played right into my stories about my insecurity. So, I would try harder to get his attention, which only created more tension. Now I see that he was acting out his own stories about love—stories which, in the end, had very little to do with me.

When your partner is emotionally wounded, or has a particularly negative love story, the relationship can become all about their needs. You may feel like you need to change, or like you're going nuts. You may find yourself rewriting a positive aspect of your story about love in order to make his behavior acceptable—but this only creates more emotional upheaval.

We can't take responsibility for someone else's love story. We can only take responsibility for our own.

Very few people naturally have the capacity for un-conditional love. Their stories are a barrier between them and their true nature. I know that I wasn't capable of unconditional love until my experience of being broken open. Only after I did the work to heal my story about love and reclaim my inner knowing of myself as a divine being was I able to step into that space for the first time. Without knowing this pain of being broken open, I would never have discovered the true nature of love. My broken heart became a badge of courage.

We'll talk more about this in the next chapter, but for now, I'll leave you with this …

REMEMBER WHO YOU *Are*

A force far greater than your human self is responsible for you being here, and that force is divine. You are a divine creation. You are a container for divine energy. You are a spiritual being having a human experience by design. Once you accept this, you will gain the power to rewrite your story in any way you choose.

Would a divine being be limited by a label like "Dumbo"? Could it even touch her? No fucking way.

The same is true for you. You don't have to live out your old stories, or anyone else's. Your old labels cannot touch you if you don't let them. If there is a reason why you were broken open, this is it. Once you know yourself as a divine being who has a choice about how to live out her life story, there's no going back. You no longer have to settle for anything less than real, true love—from yourself or anyone else.

CHAPTER FOUR

A BROKEN HEART IS A BADGE OF COURAGE

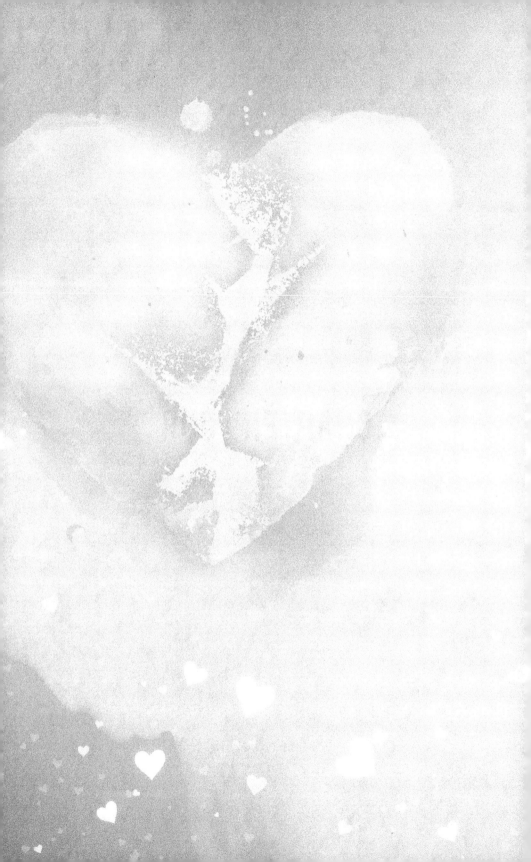

CHAPTER FOUR

A BROKEN HEART IS A BADGE OF COURAGE

"There's a crack in everything, that's how the
light gets in." - *Leonard Cohen*

$\mathcal{S}$o many women I meet express a sense of guilt or shame
over their broken hearts. The words "could have," "would
have," and "should have" are often the first out of their mouths.
They think that, if only they had done X, Y, or Z, this broken
heart would not have happened to them. They try to make the
other person's actions their fault.

It's true that it takes two to tango. Relationship dynamics
are complicated, especially when we factor in our personal
love stories. But while you *are* responsible for learning about
and shifting your personal love stories, you are *not* responsible
for the actions of the one who broke your heart open. Period.

What's done is done. There's no going back. You're finding
your way back to the path of light, and you've probably
stumbled a time or two already. You don't have to beat yourself
up on top of it.

I remember when Diane came to me for life coaching. She had recently discovered that her husband was having an affair with a woman from his office. She was so distraught that she had lost twenty pounds in just a few weeks. She couldn't eat, and barely slept. She was filled with guilt that she "caused" this to happen to her family.

I kept trying to pin down her reasoning for this. "Diane," I asked. "Why do you feel responsible for your husband's infidelity?"

Between her sobs and blowing her bright red nose, I managed to make out, "I didn't pay enough attention to his work or his interests."

"Really? You think *that* is what caused his betrayal?" It didn't sound logical.

I kept gently nudging her to explore this, and eventually discovered that she had always questioned his loyalty to her. In fact, there had been some infidelity while they were still dating. She obviously didn't feel secure in the marriage.

Diane felt that she might have pushed her husband to cheat on her because she kept "nagging him all the time." (Her words, not mine!)

Now it all made perfect sense to me. Like me, Diane had felt forewarned that her chosen prince had a wandering eye. She chose to overlook it, squelch her intuitive knowing, and get married anyway. Now, she held herself responsible for that decision. "I knew this was coming," she said. "I just thought I could stop it."

I explained that she had nothing to feel guilty about. Actually, I thought she was remarkable. She had done her best to forgive her husband for his previous indiscretions, and made a loving commitment to put the past behind them so that they could build a future together. Did she do this perfectly? Of course not. But that didn't mean that she had caused this recent cheating episode. Her husband had a history which, sadly, was repeating itself. There was a weakness in his own love story that he was acting out. This wasn't about her, but about him.

"Honey, unless you ran off with his best friend and he's screwing around for revenge, this is *not* your fault. Can you breathe that in?"

Diane laughed through her tears. "No, I didn't do anything like that."

After several sessions, Diane started to understand she didn't push her husband in any way to get involved with another woman. He chose to step outside of the marriage, knowing how much this would hurt her. Maybe she did nag him—but not every man responds to nagging with an after-hours romp on the secretary's desk.

I'm going to say it again, just so we are crystal clear: You didn't cause the actions that broke your heart open. Please, don't compound your pain with undeserved guilt.

Like you, I've worn those muddy shoes of self-condemnation. Today, however, I stand freely in greener pastures. This shift started for me when I started to look at my broken heart in a new light.

YOUR CAPACITY FOR *love*

I put everything on the line for love at the age of fifty-three.

Prior to meeting my husband, I'd been single for eighteen years. During that time, I founded and grew a fabulous real estate business and built myself a beautiful home. I also purchased a horse and competed in national competitions. I traveled the globe, and attended amazing events such as Wimbledon and the Kentucky Derby. I was focused on living a fulfilled life that didn't require a man.

I dated, of course, but no one was in my long-term vision. I actually thought I would never remarry. I was financially independent and had the resources to do as I pleased—and, in the back of my mind, I feared that getting married might change all of that.

When I first started dating my husband, marriage wasn't on my mind. I was the queen of independence. I loved my freedom. But as time went on, I started to realize that being with him was important to me, and that I might actually regret it if I didn't make a commitment. And so, I took the leap.

I recognize now that it took tremendous courage for me to get married again. I still had trust issues buried deep within my love story, but I figured I was over that. Previously, my moments of heartbreak had been fueled by my alcohol abuse. Now, I'd been in recovery for over a decade and had done a ton of inner work. I could never erase the past, but I could and did have much more powerful coping mechanisms. I figured I was safe from my old patterns.

So, I put on my confident face and plunged in. Shit, I was so self-assured that I even fooled myself.

Of course, you know already how my marriage ended—but that doesn't mean that the years I had with my husband were any less magical or meaningful. I showed up for our relationship like a gladiator in the arena, willing to take on all my fears in the name of love. To me, the glory of the fight was worth the risk of hurt and heartbreak.

When you chose love, you took a huge chance. Your broken

heart is evidence that you opened yourself up enough to be fully vulnerable to another human being. You let someone see the real you—the flawed, perfectly imperfect, totally fabulous you. Yes, it hurts now, but that doesn't mean it wasn't worth it.

YOUR PAIN IS *Evidence* OF YOUR CAPACITY FOR LOVE

Heartbreak isn't just an emotional construct. It's a real physical condition. You *feel* it throughout your body. You might be unable to eat, or you might want to eat all the time. You might be unable to sleep, or you might never want to get out of bed. You are a bundle of nerves and stress hormones, and might even slip into depression.

When you feel like love is slipping away, it's awful. Fear rushes through your body like ice and fire. Your mind automatically starts doing its "protective" thing, rolling over the situation again and again, wondering how you could have prevented this pain, and how you might be able to prevent it next time. This is normal, but when you give in to it, it will definitely drive you even deeper into panic, anxiety, depression, overwhelm, and pain.

Your pain and heartbreak are real—but your suffering? That's all in your mind.

You are creating your fear. It was born inside your thoughts, and you are feeding it with your what-ifs, your shoulds, and your might-have-beens. You push it away when you want to feel strong—but alone, in the dark, while you're crying or hugging your pillow, you stroke that fear. You scratch it between the ears. You touch it over and over to know its shape. *You keep it alive.*

61

Your ego—that nasty little voice in your head—is fear's best friend. And when fear and your ego hang out, the result is judgment. Your ego whispers about what will happen when you're vulnerable. "See what happens when you open yourself up?" it says. "You're going to get your ass kicked!"

Your mind loves to think of all the worst things that can happen. It's kind of its job; our brains evolved to keep us "safe." Your ex isn't a rampaging tiger or a hungry bear (at least, probably not), but when your body is consumed by feelings of fear, your brain can't tell the difference. It just sees a threat, and starts listing all the ways it can, should, and will deal with that threat. And when it gets going, it can be pretty convincing.

When you start judging yourself for your heartbreak, you're probably listening to your ego's persuasive dialogue. By instilling judgment and fear in you, your ego limits your choices and manipulates your actions toward the path of least resistance—the place it sees, in its twisted way, as "safety." The *really* scary thing is that, if you dwell on those fearful things and keep putting your energy behind them, you can, in fact, start to create them.

We all have that nasty little voice in our heads. The key is to recognize that the solutions it gives you might not actually be the best strategies. When in doubt, connect with your heart. Look for the light streaming through the place where you are broken open, and ask what it's trying to show you.

JOURNALING FOR COURAGE

Deep writing is one of the most therapeutic practices you can engage with when you are in the throes of crushing emotional conflict. Putting pen to paper helps to purify your soul and empty your head. It gives you the opportunity to release all the raging thoughts and see them for what they are: creations of fear or anger that are not helping you create what you actually want.

On the pages of your journal, you can let go of your pent-up feelings. You can say things that you would never normally say to another human being. It's liberating—but it also puts things in perspective.

Whenever you get overwhelmed with guilt, shame, and fear, pull out your journal. Make a quick list of everything you are feeling. What is a result of love, and what is a result of fear? Any time you can make a connection to your heart, you step closer to the truth of what you need to heal. The quick bursts of realization you get when you practice this are game-changers.

For this practice to work, you've got to be willing to wear your broken heart as a badge of courage. You've got to be willing to stare down your fear, and make choices based in love instead. Not love for the one who broke your heart open, but love for *yourself.*

During my separation and divorce, I discovered the power of writing things down. It sounds so simple to just jot down what you're feeling in any given moment, but this really did help me to see what was real, what I was creating out of fear, and what options actually existed for me. Was what I was afraid of really happening, or was it just a projection my mind was making? Was I feeling "not good enough" and blaming myself, or was I seeing the situation clearly? What needed to happen to make this situation better for *me?*

My writing gave me clarity. It showed me the truth when I was blinded by my emotions. There were times when I couldn't even see the words I'd written because I was crying so hard. But even when I was at my weakest, I held to my commitment

63

to find a positive outcome for all involved. I was *not* going to let my ego push me into becoming a scorned woman.

With a little practice, I was able to dive below my fear and start listening to my heart. And, interestingly, every time my thoughts turned to hurting my husband, or self-judgment, or feeling like a victim, I lost the thread of that connection. When I was tuned in to the hurt, I didn't have access to the same divine flow of information. The same thing happened when I tried to resist my heartbreak. When I held in the tears, or brushed off a question with, "I'm fine," my inner channel went silent.

The lesson here? Guilt and shame are unnecessary. Fear is in your mind, not your heart. And resistance is not a pathway to healing.

RESISTING YOUR *Heartbreak* IS FUTILE

If you resist your heartbreak, you give it permission to hold you hostage for a long, long time.

It's normal to have thoughts like, "I don't deserve this." But denying that it happened is foolish, and avoiding your pain can be disastrous. Sooner or later, you will have to face it—and all the damage it's done to your love story while you were busy running away.

When we are broken open, we come again to that intersection we talked about in Chapter One: You can choose the path of healing, or the path of suffering. Part of the gift of light is illumination. But you won't be able to see what the light has to show you until you accept what is there, in the darkness.

Pushing back against the heaviness of heartbreak only wears you down. Acceptance—which is really the practice of non-resistance—is your path to reclaim your power. Fear and pain are not the same thing. We avoid pain because we are afraid of it—but that road only creates more fear, and never soothes the pain. When you accept things just as they are (including your beautiful, broken-open heart), you release your ego and the fearful judgment it has created. Only then can you actually touch your pain and begin to heal it.

I met Susan at a recovery center where I was teaching a class. She had been in and out of recovery for over two decades. Each time she relapsed, she crashed and burned a little harder. She was well-educated and really smart, and honestly I was a bit bewildered by her inability to get and stay sober.

In our early discussions, we danced around the usual items that might cause a woman to drink. In my experience, these are all emotional wounds—wounds of the heart. My personal theory is that women drink because they don't feel good enough about themselves to face the world sober. I know this was true for me.

Susan was a powerful example of this. Her parents had died in a car crash when she was in her late teens. She had experienced two failed marriages, and couldn't hold a job because sooner or later she would show up drunk. She knew that she was destroying her own life, but she couldn't seem to stop.

After several weeks of conversation, we finally came to the core of Susan's pain: her resistance. She had never dealt with the crushing sadness, grief, pain, and loss she felt after her parents died, and after her marriages ended. She denied herself the experience of grieving. Instead, she tried to act as if these losses didn't affect her—as though she could simply "keep calm and carry on" through tragedy after tragedy.

Alcohol was her solution, but it was like trying to put a Band-Aid on a broken arm. The more she hid from her sadness, the

65

more she needed to drink to face her reality. The more she drank, the worse her reality became, and the more she needed to drink to hide from it. It was a terrible, vicious cycle of resistance.

Even once we identified what was happening, Susan continued to resist. As hard as I tried to help her, she refused to face her reality. After so many years of compounded pain, it was simply too much for her. She chose to continue to drink. I tried to follow up with her, but she wasn't interested, and eventually we lost touch.

Pain can be a powerful teacher, but only when we engage with it in a healthy way. My massive heartbreak inspired me to put on my big-girl pants and do the work necessary to heal my love story once and for all. I went deeper into my practices of meditation, prayer, and journaling than I ever had before. I took classes. I worked with amazing spiritual teachers who encouraged me to explore heart chakra energy and deep soul work. But the most important part of my healing was that, every time I was tempted to run from my pain, I stood and faced it. This wasn't about me being right, or needing to prove that I was bigger than what had happened to me. I needed to know who was beneath all of the fears and stories I had manufactured, because *that* was the real Mal.

The resolution that you want exists. It's within your reach, because it's within your consciousness. It only needs to be uncovered.

SELF-REALIZATION QUESTIONS

Here are some questions to help you unlock and step through your fear, resistance, shame, and guilt so you can start seeing your broken heart as a badge of courage:

- Does your partner's behavior still cause a strong, burning sense of anger when you think about it?

- Do you ever ask yourself, "Is there something I could have done better/differently to prevent this?"

- Do you ever put off feeling your emotions because they're not "convenient" or because you're afraid of where they might take you?

- Do you feel you are wiser, stronger, and more resilient for having gone through this?

- Are you doing a daily practice that empowers you and helps you to heal? If not, how can you give yourself the space to create one?

You are in a time and space of intense purification. You have to drain the infection before you can heal the wound.

Today, start giving your heart the love and credit it deserves. You gave your heart in your relationship with the best of intentions. If you hadn't, you wouldn't feel this way. You should feel proud that you loved as fully as you were able, and that you allowed yourself to be vulnerable despite the risks. You gave it all—and you can do it again.

Life and love do not come with pain-free guarantees. And really, how would you know one without the other? But even when pain is present, love is never in limited supply. You are a divine creation, and love flows through you at all times. Take some of that love and shine its light on yourself. When you fill yourself up with this light, the Universe will respond in kind. You will feel lighter, freer, and more powerful, even if your heart is still broken wide open.

So, right now, stand in front of a mirror and hug yourself. Feel the beat of your own heart. Reassure the young girl inside you that you've got this. You're courageous, brave, and capable enough to take care of both of you.

My beautiful sister, your heart is expansive and pure. Your head might be influenced by your fears, compulsions, co-dependencies, addictions, or whatever other crap you're hanging onto, but your heart is free, and its capacity for love is boundless.

So dig deep into those buried feelings. Face them head-on, and don't be afraid to ask the hard questions. Lay it all out on paper. Reread every word, and let your truth percolate in your heart not in your head. Be open to the revelations that come through fast and furious. Don't question your higher self and the answers you receive. Treat your heart like a fine instrument: tune it, nurture it, and play it with great pride. You are learning the lessons necessary to create a new, heavenly melody in your life.

CHAPTER FIVE

THERE ARE NO VICTIMS IN REAL LOVE

CHAPTER FIVE

THERE ARE NO VICTIMS IN REAL LOVE

"Our greatest errors can leave scars that become our most beautiful gifts, and our scars become reminders of grace and forgiveness." - *Mirabai Starr*

*R*eal love is freeing to your soul. You feel like you can soar like a bird, or dive as deep as a dolphin without losing your breath. You have a wonderful sense of trust and ease. Your love flows without reservation or obstacles. Most of all, you know without a doubt that, even if your whole world falls apart, love will still be there for you.

If you've experienced this kind of love, you'll know what I'm talking about. It's profound and all-encompassing. It's like an ocean of joy that you get to dip your toes into whenever you want.

Too often, though, love doesn't show up for us this way. Instead, being in love feels like being shackled to need and insecurity. It always feels like something is missing, or like we're not good enough. We're constantly trying to manipulate the object of our affections to "get" more love, or squeeze an extra drop of love from ourselves when we're already wrung dry. We become victims of love, helpless before the power our loved ones wield over us and passive in the face of ill treatment. We expect love to hurt us—and yet, we don't feel worthy of fully receiving it.

I've got a secret to share: real love will *never* leave you feeling this way. Real love comes from within you, and it will never abandon you. But when you're addicted to or dependent on love that comes from another person, you will at some point find yourself at their mercy.

When the person you counted on "getting" love from breaks open your heart, it's easy to blame them for taking love away from you. You start to see yourself as helpless in the face of their deception, and powerless over their treatment of you. This is classic victim behavior, and it's something that you will need to shift to continue on your journey of healing.

Kate is a dear client and a smart, savvy woman. However, she didn't know how to contain her anger when it came to her ex-husband. Her marriage was over; the divorce was in process. And yet, she would start unnecessary battles with her ex, over and over. She would follow him around the house when he came to pick up his belongings. When he went into another room to escape her screaming, she would just follow him. She was relentless. He would end up running out of the house to keep from getting hammered—which only meant that he had to come back again, and again. When he took shelter in his car, she would call his cell phone and keep up the barrage.

When she finally exhausted herself after these episodes, she felt like a hot mess. She would have a headache for hours, and feel totally drained. I explained to her that by projecting her anger, she was depleting herself emotionally and not gaining anything in return.

"You're right," she admitted. "Screaming at him doesn't help me. It only makes me feel like shit."

I wasn't surprised.

"These conversations make me look like an irrational beast," Kate went on. "I want to talk to him about all of this, but all I'm doing is pushing him away."

Clearly, her behavior was doing nothing for her self-esteem. It didn't help her divorce proceedings, and it didn't change the outcome. But she wasn't sure how to stop being a victim.

Over the course of our work together, Kate started to put her energy into constructive measures that brought far better results. She learned to address her ex-husband in a respectful tone of voice while still speaking her truth. She was afraid to try this at first, in case he felt like he was "getting away with it," but I reminded her that this wasn't about him. She didn't have to agree with his actions. Treating him with dignity was more about her than it was about him; it was about showing up to each interaction as the person *she* wanted to be.

Soon, she stopped getting headaches. She felt calmer, even energized, after talking to her ex. And she realized that she had the power to direct each and every conversation toward a positive outcome.

VICTIMHOOD IS *Not* A COPING STRATEGY

Chances are, if you're feeling victimized by your broken heart, your love story has something to do with it.

Listen when statements like, "I can't believe he did this to me" or "I did everything for him" pass your lips.

When you're in a victim state, you may be preoccupied with what you think you deserve but aren't getting; this means that you're not able to look objectively at what is actually happening. You paint a picture of yourself as a martyr to love, continually making sacrifices at the altar of your relationship. You want to keep repeating a story of unbearable injustice so that everyone around you will feel your pain. If you don't pull yourself out of this, you will stay stuck in your negative story. Commiserating with others will become the only way you know how to communicate about love. And you will never heal your broken heart.

It's time to recognize that the story coming from your wounded self may be far from the truth. You can't take responsibility for someone else's feelings, beliefs, or actions—but you *can* take responsibility for your own. That means that everything you think, feel, and do is yours and yours alone.

There is a lesson you need to learn. It's up to you to identify the wounded patterns that you need to heal—but before you do so, you have to admit that this healing is, and always has been, within your power.

By blaming another person for your broken heart, or making them responsible for your life and well-being, you are not helping yourself. Blame and victimhood are just another way of resisting your pain. However, by making your pain someone else's problem, you're not giving it away. It doesn't get thrust on the person who hurt you. You're only fooling yourself.

When you give away your pain, you also give away your power. If you can't take responsibility for your broken heart, you can't take responsibility for mending it. You can't take responsibility for your healing. And, ultimately, this means you can't take responsibility for your happiness.

Stepping out of victimhood allows you to step into the reality of what is happening both inside of you and in your life circumstances. You can put aside the persona of the damsel in distress, the loved one who has been unjustly mistreated. You can let go of your judgments about the one who hurt you and take the first steps toward forgiveness.

If your first thought after reading that last line was, "I'll never forgive him," I get it. You're in pain, sister. Your heart is cracked open. But really, is that judgment getting you anywhere? How can you find solutions when you're not willing to get off your pedestal and start looking for them?

Self-righteousness is the greatest block to conscious awareness that exists for human beings. The need to be "right" at all costs is like poison to our souls, because it blinds us to both potential solutions and our power to create them. Awareness weakens our internal conflicts so we can begin the healing process. The more we can release our thoughts of right and wrong, the more easily we can get to a neutral state of what *is*; from there, we can build.

In other words, we can't build a new home on ground that's still being bombed—especially if we're the ones doing the bombing.

I'm sure you can think of a time when you've kept fighting over something long after the actual event was over. It's easy to get caught up in that crazy need to have the last word, the final gut punch that knocks your opponent over. It's also easy to want to possess, control, or give too much because you think you can get something in return. But all of those battle tactics take *energy*. (Think of Kate with her headaches!) That energy now needs to

75

be put elsewhere: into growing, healing, and moving on.

Surrendering to what is allows us to see what can be. When you surrender, you're not turning into a doormat; in fact, you're taking your first step toward reclaiming your power.

As I've shared, I had a disastrous relationship history prior to my marriage. Several of the significant loves in my life broke my heart with betrayal. I would give and give and give, always trying to be what I thought the other person wanted—and I ended up settling for crumbs.

For a while, especially while I was still abusing alcohol, this was *primo* fuel for victim behavior. I would sob in misery, "Why doesn't he love me? How could he do this to me?" But once I got sober and started doing some serious inner work, I finally started to see the patterns that had haunted my love life since Mitch broke my heart in my early twenties.

The problem wasn't the men who kept breaking my heart. The problem was with me.

The men I'd loved hadn't hurt me because I was weak and at their mercy. They'd hurt me because I had *given them my power*, and made myself powerless in the relationship. They couldn't help but hurt me. I was a doormat waiting to be stepped on.

Obviously, my drinking had affected the choices I made and what I was willing to put up with. However, this went far deeper than that. *How I felt about myself* was causing my heartache.

If I didn't value myself, how could I expect someone else to value me? And if I gave away my power over and over, how could I expect to feel anything but powerless?

It took years of work in my recovery as well as many books, classes, and women's retreats to finally accept that I was worthy and deserving of happiness. Once I flipped that switch,

I found a piece of my life's calling: coaching other women and helping them heal from heartbreak. Working with other women reinforced everything I had learned and strengthened my own worth and sense of purpose.

I thought I had it figured out completely, and I felt really good about myself. Then, I decided to get married to a man I talked myself into trusting completely. I believed we were soul mates, twin flames, destined to be together. I wanted this to be true so badly that I ignored my gut feelings and swallowed the questions that made me look insecure. My soul kept trying to speak to me, but I chose not to listen. Once again, in a subtle but undeniable way, I had compromised my self-worth for a man.

The fact that I made this choice was no one's fault but mine. And if I wanted to heal and move on, I couldn't pull the "poor me" bullshit anymore. I had to own this, and do what it took to heal it, if I wanted to stop this pattern once and for all.

What I discovered, as I poured these revelations into my journal, was that I had a deep pattern of not trusting people, masked with a naïve willingness to believe in them anyway. My big takeaway was that the balance or outcome of every relationship I've ever had was predicated on my feelings about myself, and not the other person's behavior.

Admitting and accepting that my patterns and beliefs about myself led to my experience of being broken open didn't mean that I was okay with what my husband had done; in fact, it strengthened my resolve that what he had done was wrong on many, many levels. But I had *allowed* those wrongs to be done to me. I had fed my fears in the night. I kept telling myself faulty stories about my insecurity and worthiness. I didn't have to own my husband's actions, but I did need to own my allowing of them. Until I did, I was going to keep living the same old love story over and over.

The crack in my heart had been trying to show me this truth for decades. Finally, I had been broken open wide enough to see it. It felt like getting a piece of shrapnel pulled from my heart. It hurt—but now I could bleed freely, and heal cleanly.

WHAT HAPPENS WHEN YOU *Stop* PLAYING THE VICTIM

Sasha is a truly beautiful woman who kept getting her heart ripped out by the same man.

The story went something like this: her man would charm her and woo her, telling her all the right things. She would fall into his arms. Several months later, though, he would get nudgy and take off, leaving her alone and consumed with grief. Then, weeks or months later, he'd come back around, and the cycle would begin again.

Sasha was consumed with grief. She wasn't even enjoying the "ups" of her up-and-down relationship anymore. Her health was starting to deteriorate. Worst of all, she blamed herself for her boyfriend's actions. She came from a very traditional Middle-Eastern family where women were not valued, and she believed that it was simply her destiny to be treated this way.

I was blown away by this. Honestly, her story brought me to tears. Sasha was gorgeous, brilliant, and had a prolific career. She was working on multiple graduate degrees in her specialty. Her English was flawless, her accent mesmerizing. She was completely clueless as to how sensual she looked and sounded.

We worked together for a while, focusing on all the things she had been able to accomplish in her life, and building out her new online business. When I said she needed to have a website in order to launch an online business, she responded, "I can't do that! My whole family will see me online. How will I explain to them what I am doing?"

"Maybe they'll see that you're trying to build a business around the fifteen degrees you're paying loans for!" I suggested.

I wanted to help her shift her focus onto things she could do that (probably) wouldn't terrorize her family but would still boost her self-esteem and help her create an income. She was extraordinarily talented, but completely insecure. And this boyfriend situation wasn't helping her at all.

We took a deep dive into her inner work over the next several months. She stopped speaking to the itinerant boyfriend and put all of her energy into her own healing. When she felt ready, we spent a VIP day together looking at the stories she was telling herself about herself. She had come to realize how deeply she believed that, as a woman, she was inherently worthless. All the education in the world wouldn't shift that belief for her unless she chose to tell herself a different story—a story she wrote for herself.

After that day, Sasha was like a different person. She felt confident. She believed in herself and her worth. And she made choices that made her feel fulfilled, instead of catering to what she perceived her family would want for her.

The changes in her life over the next year were remarkable. Her family slowly got on board with what she was doing, even came to support her. She completed two Master's degrees. And the man who kept leaving her and breaking her heart came back around for the last time … and asked her to marry him.

Sasha's story is a perfect example what can happen when you step out of victimhood and into empowerment.

Her journey wasn't easy. She had to release a lot of fear to uncover the love within her—and that meant facing a lot of things she'd been avoiding, and rewriting big scenes in her personal love story. But she was willing to do the work, because the alternative was unacceptable to her. And in the end, she got her fairy tale.

One of the practices that I did with Sasha was something I call "Fear Finding." Fear always has physical side effects. By tuning into where the fear lives in your body, you can actually move through it in a sensory way, rather than getting caught up in your mind.

When you start to notice that you are in a state of fear, get to a private place as soon as you can (even if it's the restroom at work). Close your eyes and take a few deep breaths. See if you can discover where the fear is lodged in your body. Then, breathe into that area as you ask yourself these questions.

- "What do I fear?"

- "What will happen if this fear comes to pass?"

- "What are the chances that this will actually happen?"

It's best if you can work with these questions in your journal, but if that's not possible, do it in your head. This inquiry will help you realize that, most likely, you are not fearing something real, only projecting into the future.

Once you have your answers, bring yourself back to your breath. Remember that you are in the present moment. Your fear isn't happening right now; it's only in your mind. You have faced it, and let it teach you. Now, it's time to let it go. Close your eyes and ask for guidance about the best way to do this.

SELF-REALIZATION QUESTIONS

- What is your biggest fear about the situation you are going through?

- Where does your fear lead you to feel victimized or powerless?

- What would you be willing to do to put all of this behind you?

- Do you actually want an outcome that is highest and best for you?

- What would change if you actually felt powerful in this situation?

- What have you learned about yourself from going through this?

Once you've answered these questions, make a list of all the things you say, write, or think on a regular basis that play into victim energy. For example, you might write down a thought like, "I sacrificed everything for him. How could he do this to me?" or "I'll never be good enough for anyone again." If you're not sure which of your thoughts are victim thoughts, tune into your body as you say them out loud. Victim thoughts will make you feel smaller, compressed, tight, or in pain. It may be hard to take a deep breath. On the other hand, thoughts that are liberating will make you feel expansive, light, and buoyant, and will help you breathe more easily.

Now, take all of your victim statements and flip them around so that they become more empowering. For example, "How could he do this me?" might become "What do I need to

81

heal so that this never happens again?" And "I'll never be good enough" might become "I am healing my heart so I can fully experience love."

When we are stuck in a victim mentality, we feel both unloved and unable to fully give love, because we believe love is conditional. We have to get it, withhold it, take it from someone else. Well, sister, that's bullshit—and now you know it.

Each and every woman on this planet is capable of loving and being loved unconditionally. Your broken heart is the gateway to your power. It is showing you the way to heal your victim mindset and stop it from corrupting your love story. If you are willing to step up to the plate and do the work, the rewards will be bigger than you could ever imagine.

CHAPTER SIX

THOUGHTS COMPLICATE LOVE

CHAPTER SIX

THOUGHTS COMPLICATE LOVE

"Your task is not to seek for love, but merely to seek and
find all the barriers within yourself that you have built
against it." - *Rumi*

*L*ove is unconditional, universal, and available to all of us. But when our love stories start to develop, it's like we put blinders on. We start to see love as only possible in certain ways, at certain times, and from certain people. Add in those damaging stories we tell ourselves about our worth and lovability, and you have a recipe for some pretty messed-up shit.

When we first fall in love, it's like life is magical. You are unstoppable, flying high on cloud nine. And since you believe this is how it's "supposed to be," you roll with it. In fact, you might be so addicted to the rush of it that you ignore anything that doesn't point you in that direction of bliss—including signals from your heart and soul. But that rush can't last. Just like every drunken night comes with a painfully sober morning, eventually you come down from the high and have to deal with reality. And often, that reality doesn't match up with your expectations. This is where suffering begins.

In Chapters Two and Three, we started to get in touch with your love story and peel back the layers of misinformation to get to who you truly are at your core. Then, we talked about wearing your broken heart as a badge of courage, and how stepping out of victimhood can lead you back to your power. Now, we're going to go deeper, to where all of your joy and your suffering begin: your thoughts.

As we've explored, the love that most of us experience is narrowed and boxed in by a set of conditions: our love story, which we formed as children based on how love was given to, or withheld, from us. We have expectations around what someone who loves us will and won't do, what they will and won't say. When those conditions aren't met, we become very uncomfortable. We start to judge ourselves, and the one we love. We start to try to change ourselves, or the other person. We start to manipulate, hide, even outright lie. These are the conditions which often lead up to being broken open. For one reason or another, we aren't accepting things as they are; instead, we're wishing they were different, or better.

Love is blind at first because you're euphoric. You're not thinking, you're feeling. But the longer you spend in love with an unhealed love story, the greater the chance that these conditions and unmet expectations will surface—and the more likely you will be to let your thoughts run away with them.

You start to think things like, "If he really loved me, he would change." Or, "If I was good enough, he wouldn't treat me like this." Your ego, whose job it is to rationalize the irrational and keep you safe, provides reasons why your reality doesn't match up with your expectations—reasons that play right into your fears, like, "Maybe he doesn't love me enough to change," or, "Maybe he does love me, and I actually deserve to get treated like this." These thoughts lead you into a spiral of compensating, wishing, and ignoring the truth that your heart is trying to speak.

Love isn't subject to your thoughts. It will exist no matter what you think about it. But your *experience* of love is 100 percent subject to your beliefs. And until you heal that old love story, those same old wounds will just keep opening up.

In the past, up to and including when I met my husband, I always started off in a new relationship feeling like I was levitating. I would build up the relationship in my thoughts to epic, storybook levels—only to crash all the harder when I came back to Earth. I never looked at what was, only what I *wanted* things to be. I would talk myself into sudden rapture, and allow myself to be swept off my feet without any clue as to the man's intentions or character. I wanted them to prove to me that I was worthy of love—and yet, my deeply-buried love story said I couldn't trust them, that they would betray me.

I was deliberately running blind, letting my thoughts spiral out of control. In fact, I started to notice that the more insatiable I felt about someone, the more likely it was that I was in for a massive disappointment.

Even knowing this, I kept launching myself into love like a circus performer from a cannon. Hey, you can't knock a girl for trying.

ARE YOU *Thinking* ABOUT WHAT IS, OR WHAT MIGHT BE?

After Mitch broke my heart open for the first time, I stumbled through a series of disastrous relationships. One in particular was with a man I'll call Alan. He was twenty-two years older than me, and I thought he was the greatest, sexiest, most attractive man who had ever walked the earth. He was also masterful at manipulating young women, including me.

For a few months, I basked in the glow of Alan's affection. I was his primary target ... until someone better came along.

During our affair, I felt like a ping-pong ball. I never knew what to expect. I bounced from elation to depression and back again, sometimes in the space of a single hour. He would be with me one day, gone the next, and then back again like nothing had happened. Every time he reappeared, he would sweep me off my feet again, only to drop me on the pavement.

I wanted to believe in him. Thinking he was a total liar was simply too painful for me. My thoughts were torn between my fears of being unlovable and my delusions of what being loved looked like. If only I could make him see that I was the one he needed!

Finally, I decided to show up at his place in the middle of the night, unannounced. He'd told me he was sick and going to bed early, but I needed to know what was really going on. I guess I needed to see it to believe it.

I walked right into his bedroom—and there he was, tangled up with another woman. A lot of screaming from three totally crazed people ensued.

Yes, I had a *lot* of drama in my younger years, especially when I was drinking. But most of the time, the damage our thoughts do to us, and to our relationships, is much more subtle. For example, have you ever thought, "He doesn't dote on me like my dad doted on my mom. He must not love me as much as my parents loved one another." Or, "He always falls asleep when we're watching a movie. What's his problem? Doesn't he care that I'm here?" Or, "He doesn't bring me tiny bags with tinier lacy bits inside anymore. Doesn't he find me attractive anymore?" Yes, maybe your partner is doing these things. But your thoughts about them are not helping the issue. In fact, they're distorting reality, because you're comparing what is to what you think "should" be. More and more, you spend your time thinking about what's wrong, and not what's right.

How different would your experience be if you simply allowed whatever was happening, and made choices from there? What if you relaxed your conditions and your rules, and gave up on all the "shoulds"?

You can't manipulate love on the other side of a relationship. You can only work with your half of it. The words you choose create the thoughts you have about love, and about the person you love. Those same thoughts control your feelings. Your thoughts can trash real love if you're not careful.

When you've been broken open, your thoughts can easily go off the deep end. You might be thinking, "He's with someone else," even if there's no evidence to prove that. You might be feeling abandoned. You might be wondering how the hell you will survive on your own after so long in a partnership. There's a ton of crazy, painful stuff running around in your mind. These thoughts, and the feelings of abandonment, rage, and powerlessness they create, can lead you to do things that you wouldn't normally do—things you might later regret. Then, not only has your pain not gone away, your thoughts hop on the shame train, where they can do even more damage.

If this sounds familiar, your thoughts might be out of control. The key when you're in that place is not to assume anything. In fact, *everything* you think or assume should be suspect right now. Write everything out in your journal, try to stay calm, and allow time for the truth to surface. In time, you will get the clarity you're craving. Chances are, it will bring with it some major revelations and healing lessons.

I often recommend that women in negative thought spirals go away for a weekend to clear out and reset their minds. If that's not possible, a relaxing spa treatment, or even a day unplugged at the park or the beach will help. If you still can't get a handle on your mind, talk with a professional therapist or psychiatrist. I can say from experience that therapy really does help.

OUR THOUGHTS *Fuel* OUR TROUBLES

I think we can agree that I've been real with you about my struggles with addictions and failed relationships, right? But here's the point I want to drive home: While I don't blame myself for Alan's behavior, or Mitch's, or my husband's, I do recognize that most of my troubles were fueled, if not outright created, by my own repetitive thoughts.

This is a huge admission, and one that took me many years to make. However, when I owned that my thoughts were the culprit in so many of my disasters, including my alcohol addiction, I was finally able to change them—and change my experience of love in the bargain.

On December 30, 1988, I was at the crossroads of life and death. I had been in a downward spiral of negative thinking and drinking for years. I drank so I wouldn't feel the pain of feeling worthless, but the things I did and said while I was drunk created drama after drama. Every day, there was more pain and shame to run from—so every day, I drank more. I started to believe that death would be preferable to the hell I was living.

On this day, I started thinking about the new year. I was supposed to go to a New Year's Eve party, which I knew would be a disaster since I couldn't control my drinking. Even drunk, I'd feel alone, abandoned, like a freak. And then, it would be 1989. I couldn't live through another year like this. I wasn't even sure I could live another day. I just couldn't shove away these feelings of worthlessness again. I didn't have it in me. The walls were closing in, and I was just so tired of it all.

I curled up on my bed in a ball of agony, pulled the covers over my face, and totally surrendered to my pain. I let it flood into me, let it fill me up like a burning flame. "I could just let go," I thought. "I have some Xanax. If I took it all, and drank the rest of that vodka …"

Then, another voice spoke in my head. "Oh dear child, you can't leave now!"

What the hell? I poked my head out from under the covers, wondering who else was in the room with me.

The voice continued, "You have much work to do. You have many lessons to learn, and when you have mastered those lessons, you will need to go and teach others. You have an amazing life ahead of you, and much to do on my behalf. It is time to put an end to your suffering."

A feeling of peace came over me. My fear dropped away. I knew in that instant that I wasn't crazy; I was having a spiritual awakening after a long, dark night of the soul.

This was my first experience of the healing that can come when we allow the light to reach our broken places.

I staggered to the bathroom, wondering if I would see a completely different woman—but I still looked like the same walking disaster. Swollen face, red eyes, nose runny from sobbing.

91

And yet, I felt different. God had spoken to me, and I was ready to listen. For the first time in ages, I didn't feel disgusted by the woman I saw looking back at me. In fact, I felt deep compassion for her.

"What have you been doing to yourself, girl?" I thought.

At the crack of dawn, I got dressed and ran to my neighbor George's house. George was a sponsor in Alcoholics Anonymous, and for months he'd been telling me that he was holding a chair for me at the meetings. On this New Year's Eve morning, I told him that I was ready to sit in it.

I started 1989 as a sober woman. Nearly thirty years later, I am still in recovery.

A few months into my sobriety, everything started coming to the surface. I made a startling revelation: while the people in my life had done some awful things, it was my own poisonous thinking which had caused most of my suffering. I had been blaming everyone else for my misery, but it was my thoughts that kept me tethered to my emotional pain.

My repetitive thoughts about events that had happened so long ago—for example, Mitch's betrayal, or that haunting "Dumbo" comment—created my feelings of unworthiness and fueled my self-destructive behavior. My life was defined by my past. I had been holding on to every painful word, every disastrous relationship, replaying them over and over. It was like every time life knocked me down, I kept punching myself in the same spot over and over, keeping the pain fresh, making sure I was still bleeding. It was no wonder I couldn't heal and move on!

My first thought was, "Why the hell would I do that to myself?" The second thought was, "Holy shit. I can fix this … because I *created* it!"

That was the moment where my real transformation began.

I worked really hard to recover myself. I read the right books, took classes, and worked with various coaches. I stepped into a whole new arena of self-love and self-respect.

And then, after eighteen years of being sober and single, I met my husband, and a good chunk of it went out the window. I was back to being insecure, questioning my heart's wisdom, and listening to the same thoughts on repeat in my head. It wasn't as traumatic as it had once been; it was more like it played beneath the surface, when I wasn't paying attention. As I've shared, this led me to make choices against my inner knowing. I ended up broken open again—and this time, the crack was wide and deep enough for me to see all the skeletons I'd left hidden in the corners.

STILLNESS IS THE *Answer*

What helped me most this time around was the abilities I'd cultivated in the years since I got sober—in particular, the ability to simply sit still and be present with whatever I'm thinking and feeling.

Almost every day, I start my morning with at least a half-hour of deep breathing, meditation, and journaling. This is my way of being conscious of my thoughts. It is amazing what I can uncover when my mind isn't running wild, and how easy it is to change my thoughts when I drag them into the light.

One of my biggest takeaways from this practice is that we are not defined by past mistakes. In the eyes of God, we are fully loved in this present moment, and in all moments. Knowing this, I can release all the guilt and shame that once controlled me, and step into a space of loving compassion for myself.

(Most of the thoughts that hurt us are thoughts of judgment.) As we covered in Chapter Five, judgment is what happens when fear and ego get in bed together. Judgment distorts your reality because, like victimhood, it doesn't want to accept what is. If you really want to heal and work through a difficult situation, you have to put your judgments aside. *All* of them.

Judgment doesn't allow you to access what you're feeling because it tries to justify only one side—your side. You are not able to work toward anything, because judgment keeps you separated from everything. Meditation and mindful breathing bring your attention fully back to yourself, which is what you need when you feel broken and fragmented. The more awareness you develop, the faster you will be able to set aside your judgments, step out of conflict, and see things clearly. You can pull your thoughts, your feelings, and all the shattered pieces back together into a shape that holds love in a whole new way.

Being conscious of your breath is one of the best ways to still your thoughts and become more present. Your breath is your life force, and it connects you to your spiritual body— aka, your soul. When you breathe in, you're connecting with the divine. When you breathe out, you're releasing all that no longer serves you.

Here is one of my favorite exercises for releasing judgment and coming into stillness:

- Sit quietly in a place where you won't be interrupted.

- Inhale deeply into your lower belly, expanding your belly as you breathe in for a count of four.

- Hold your breath for a count of four.

- Exhale for a count of four, pulling your low belly back and in as you do.

- Repeat for three to five minutes.

This simple breathing exercise balances the energy that is flowing through your body, and soothes your raw emotions. When you are finished with the breathing exercise, ask yourself, "What do I need to do for myself today to keep feeling peaceful?" Ask the same question over and over for about ten minutes, and write down your answers. What comes up may surprise you.

It's so easy to hold on to the thoughts you create—to the bits and pieces of memory and experience you string together to form your love story. (Your patterns—including your thoughts—are formed from these shards of your past, not from the present moment.) You end up filtering your current experience through your old thoughts and previous traumas. (When you use an exercise like the one above to "interrupt" your thought patterns, you break the chain and allow something new to be placed in the open space.)

Fear distorts the best of circumstances and only highlights what's not right. Meditation and journaling together are the fastest pathway to what is in your heart (A daily practice allows you to access your higher spiritual self, push the mental chaos aside and hear the gentle song coming from your soul. It is a blissful return to the unconditional love that you were born with, the love that is pure, un-opinionated, and honest. You arrived on this glorious planet as a clean slate, not knowing fear, hate, anger, and loss.) Your family domestication and life experiences have taught you the meaning of these words and how to add your personal perception to everything. Each time you feel hurt you add another filter to the way you look at things. By applying these filters, you feel it's a way of protecting yourself in the future. Unfortunately, each layer that you add pushes you one step further from the truth. Your vision becomes completely clouded over by what you think is real.

SELF-REALIZATION QUESTIONS

- What are your habitual thoughts about love?
- Can you recognize where your thinking may be causing your pain?
- How are your thoughts contributing to your judgments about yourself and others?
- What thoughts are you willing to change in order to experience yourself and your story differently?
- How can you think of yourself and your life with greater compassion today?

ARE YOU READY TO *Learn?*

Life is a classroom, and all of our experiences—especially the painful ones—are lessons. Pain is a great warning sign. It means you're heading in the wrong direction. If your thoughts and beliefs about yourself or anyone else cause you pain, it's time to change them.

Now, when I've experienced something upsetting, or when my thoughts start to run away from me, I look for the lesson. I ask myself, "What do I need to take away from this? How did I participate in this situation?" The more deeply I question myself, the more clarity I get. Instead of feeling like I got fucked over, I feel like I have full power to make choices aligned with the wisdom of my heart. I take ownership, and don't make excuses. As a result, I never feel squeezed into only one option, and I know I can rely on myself to do the right thing—the thing most aligned with love—in every circumstance, even the most painful.

Being in love is yummy. Being in love with yourself is even *better* than yummy. It's total bliss. When you release the judgments you're holding about your relationship, your ex, and yourself for being broken open, you invite love to fill that space inside you. And if you allow love to help you change your thoughts, you'll create an irresistible magnetic field that will draw in—you guessed it—more love.

Feeling the energy of love, whether it comes from inside you or is expressed to you by another, is part of your divine birthright. You are not here to suffer, but instead to flourish and experience immense joy. Love and connection are fundamental to your health and happiness. The only thing standing in the way is your *thinking*, because (as we've learned in this chapter) your thoughts about love create your experience of it.

So, right now, release the old judgments, stories, and thought patterns that are feeding your toxic love story, and make room in your heart for the new concepts I'm going to share with you in the rest of this book. Surrender the feelings that you don't need so that you can be open and free to receive unconditional love.

Remember, no matter what your thoughts tell you, there is no good or bad love. There's no one who deserves love more than someone else. There's no way to get love, or earn love, or be better so that you can be loved.

There's just love.

CHAPTER SEVEN

WASHING AWAY YOUR OLD LOVE STORY

CHAPTER SEVEN

"It is your personal story that you need to awaken from in order to be free." - *Adyashanti*

*H*ave you ever had a really bad hairdo? You leave the salon and run home, screaming like a madwoman, and jump in the shower as fast as you can? You're frantic, thinking, "I'm ruined!"

That is, until you get out of the shower, redo your hair, and see that your new 'do is actually okay. Maybe even better than okay.

Rewriting your personal love story is a bit like that.

Right now, after looking at your thoughts and patterns and unhelpful beliefs about love, you might feel a bit unmoored. You've said to your stylist—who, in this case, is your higher self—"Cut it all off!" And she did.

Now, you might be freaking out. Your old way of being is gone, but you haven't gotten comfortable with a new way of being yet. It's okay. It always takes a couple of applications of surrender before you can release your old love story fully, and start to write a new one. You're washing away years, maybe even decades, of heartbreaking crud.

That's a lot of shampoo, girl.

Let's simplify what you can do to help yourself right now. You know that most of what you think and feel about love and relationships is coming from your beliefs—your love story, the experiences of your childhood and young adulthood, and your false beliefs about what love is (or should be).

When you start to wash those old beliefs away, self-doubt often sets in. You start to question whether letting go of that old love story is the right thing to do. After all, it fit you so well, at the time …

This moment, right now, is crucial. You've widened the crack in your heart enough to see where your old love story was hurting you. Maybe you've even started to do some healing—metaphorically, you've chosen to cut all that heavy old hair off. On your way to the salon, you start to feel a little better, a little lighter. But you're also in a danger zone.

Right now, it's like you're in the middle of the shampoo. Your stylist is washing all the buildup out of your old hairdo. You're feeling so much better, knowing that some of the crud is gone—but you're still questioning your decision to go all the way, and get rid of that old hairdo for good.

At this moment, you're in orbit around choice. You can say, "Okay, I get it. My old love story sucked. But I'm all cried out, and I feel better now." It's tempting to say, "That's far enough," and keep your old ways of being. So often, when those scissors come out, we end up wimping out and saying, "Just a little off the ends, please."

Why would someone back down in the middle of a transformation, especially one that could transform their old love story of suffering and pain?

Part of it is fear of the unknown. We don't know who we are without our awful old love stories. We can't see who we will be in this new expression of ourselves, and so we choke at the last minute.

Part of it, though, is those old, deep-rooted fears and judgments we still hold about what it means to love and be loved.

Up until now, we've concentrated mostly on your personal love story, and how your ideas about who you are and what you deserve ultimately create the love scenes in your personal story. But there's one more piece of your love story that will always rear its ugly head when those metaphorical scissors come out: the judgments of others.

We might hear—in our heads or out of the mouths of others—things like:

- "In my day, people worked it out. They didn't get divorced."

- "A man will never respect you if …"

- "You couldn't keep your man happy? What's wrong with you?"

- "You can't possibly *want* to be single!"

- "If someone loves you, they should always …"

Chances are, these statements aren't even really coming from you. They're simply implants left over from your old love story. And yet, once you've worked through some of your pain and broken-heartedness, and your new life and love story are starting to become visible on the horizon, these old conventions and conversations might arise to trip you up.

They might tell you, in their snide voices, why you're on the wrong path, and why these new ideas you're learning about love and self-love are bullshit. They might say things like, "Who do you think you are?" and "That's not the way things work."

The key is not to wince when the scissors come out. When these old fears arise, recognize that they're part of your past, not part of your future. Your new love story doesn't have to follow these old, outdated plots. So instead of taking them in as truth, sit with each of them and work out a new response.

For example, if you keep hearing, "In my day, people worked it out. They didn't get divorced," you might say (or write), "It's more important to me to be happy than to be married."

If your trigger is, "A man will never respect you if ..." you might reply, "The more I respect myself, the more I will be respected ... by everyone."

If you're hearing, "You failed! You couldn't keep your man happy!" you might respond with a statement like, "The only person whose happiness I am responsible for is *me*."

When you do this, you're telling yourself part of your new love story. Use your journaling time to respond constructively to judgments like the ones above. And, if you're actually hearing these statements from people in your life, use the responses you've created to hold your ground.

The words you choose around your new love story will either cripple or empower you. Often, you don't even realize how much of that old internal dialogue you're holding on to until you put it on paper. I did this myself when, in the early stages of my divorce, I was fearful about the proceedings and what everyone would have to say about my choices. I was bracing myself for a wave of anger and judgment. But when I got clear on what I wanted my new story to be around these issues, my way of being with them changed. As I wrote every day, my language started to change. My words softened. I started to ease into this new version of me—the me who focused on feeling good and healing my heart.

Your journaling practice is one of the best ways to keep yourself on track as you move through this stage of your healing process. Use your writing to wake up to what doesn't feel right inside, and choose words and actions that help you feel better.

YOUR *love* PERSONALITY

Another thing that's helpful to do at this point in your healing process is to look objectively at your "love personality." You've done a lot of work to get underneath the painful, charged parts of your story, so you should be able to see pretty clearly what category (or categories) you fall into on this spectrum.

THE GIVER

The Giver is the woman who feels like she has to earn love. She gives so much that there is nothing left inside for her. She can also be very vocal about how much she gives, sounding almost bitter at times—but her discomfort with over-giving doesn't make her stop doing it. In fact, the more people listen, the more she might talk about how much she does for others, and how little she gets in return.

The Giver may have grown up in a home where her mother

105

scarified everything for her family, or where high expectations were placed on her at a very young age. She craves the feeling of being loved and valued, but the only way she knows how to get it is to give everything she has, and more, keeping nothing back for herself.

If you are a Giver, when conflict arises, your tendency is to want to overcompensate; instead, do less, so you can place your energy selectively. Pull your energy and focus back into yourself, so you can see exactly where you are bleeding out. Where have you sacrificed your own needs on the altar of your relationship? Where have you made choices that go against your values, or your own best interests?

THE NEEDER

The Needer is the woman who must be in a relationship at all costs. If she doesn't have a man, she doesn't feel complete. She will tolerate cruel behavior, even outright abuse, and usually ends up being treated like a doormat. Then, she wonders what happened, and where she went wrong.

The Needer was raised on a diet of "shoulds." She *should* get married. She *should* want a husband and children more than anything else in the world. She *should* be satisfied with the fact that she is "marriage material," and never hope for anything more. Often, Needers come from families who are socially sheltered, traditional, and/or highly religious. Their self-worth is predicated on marital status and their status in their church.

Have you been holding yourself back in areas of your life like career, education, or self-development because you've been focused on finding or keeping a man? Have you been prioritizing finding a new relationship over healing your broken heart? Where do you feel weaker when you are not in a relationship?

Often, Needers don't self-identify right away. So if there's even the slightest doubt in your mind that you might have these tendencies, spend time with the above questions. Your independence can only be developed through your own effort, and until you recognize where you are holding yourself back, you will never be clear about what you actually want.

THE TAKER

Takers look for a partner with financial assets and status. They don't marry for love as much as they do for security and social connection. Then, they get bored with all the material stuff and start wondering where to look for real, passionate love.

Takers are often raised in homes that are either very wealthy or very poor. They are driven to marry for security either because that's what they are used to, or because that's what they felt was denied to them growing up. Either way, their relationships are often very shaky. When their significant others betray them, they often look the other way because they don't want to jeopardize their comfortable life—even as their self-worth is being flushed down the toilet.

If your partner's career, looks, money, or possessions are more important to you than the way he treats you, you might be a Taker. Don't be ashamed of this. There are many reasons why you may have played the part of a Taker in your old love story. Now that you are aware, though, it's time to ask, "What am I *not* willing to sacrifice for money and prestige?" This is the first step to reclaiming your inner integrity and setting healthy boundaries.

THE ALLOWER

The Allower puts her man on a pedestal. She loves deeply, but can easily be blinded by that love, and so she excuses or ignores all kinds of bad behavior. She doesn't complain much, and avoids confrontation. However, she has a threshold—and when that line is crossed, look out! When William Congreve wrote his lines, "Hell hath no fury like a woman scorned," he had Allowers in mind.

Allowers were often raised in homes where Daddy was king, and his needs superseded everyone else's. If she was lucky, the Allower was Daddy's little princess; if not, she always felt like she wasn't enough.

When your own worthiness is not well-defined, it's easy to idolize a man instead of demanding that he love you in a healthy way. However, when you make a man the center of your world, you really do make him king. Everything rests on him—including your happiness. Understandably, most men don't like being put in that position; your partner shouldn't be responsible for your happiness any more than you are responsible for his. Those men who do like Allower behavior tend to take full advantage—as so many of my exes did.

***

It is important for you to know your Love Personality because, as you begin to rewrite your love story in the second half of this book, you'll want to pay attention to whether you're showing up as the same old character in this new version of your movie.

Chances are, you've already noticed how your Love Personality was derived from your early family relationships and models of love. Maybe one or more of the examples above were even accurate for you. Try not to judge yourself (or your parents) for having these tendencies. They are what they are—but they no longer need to define the role you play in your own love story.

The good news is, understanding that you have these tendencies allows you to make conscious choices to change them. Understanding how you operate gives you the power to do something different. Seeing old patterns allows you to break them.

Every morning during my divorce, I did my journaling. Often, I would ask God for clarity. "Please show me the truth so I can do the right thing," I'd pray. I soon realized that I was a combination of a Giver and an Allower. When I held these archetypes up to my past relationships, I almost gagged. How many times had I put a man on a pedestal, and ended up feeling inferior to them even though they were the ones doing messed-up stuff? How many times had I given, and given in, even when it was clear that the relationship was almost over? How many times had I created insane scenarios just to get to see my "prince" one more time?

Far too many, as it turns out.

While I was modeling, I would get access to some of the most amazing events in the world. One ploy I used a lot was to use my access to bring a man to an expensive, exciting sports or music event. "Once he sees what I can do for him," the Giver in me reasoned, "he'll want to be with me forever!"

A perfect example was the celebrity tennis match in Boston with Billy Jean King and other high-profile players. White Stag sportswear was a sponsor, and since I was modeling for them, I got to be a ball girl. My relationship at the time was fizzling out, but I figured I could save it by bringing him along to this star-studded event. He was a major tennis buff, and I couldn't think of a better way to impress him than to get him a VIP seat at this event.

Boy, was that a mistake.

There were other models everywhere, not to mention all the preppy, ponytailed female tennis enthusiasts. I could immediately see that my boyfriend was on the prowl. He was hitting on practically everyone, regardless of the fact that I was standing right there! I got so caught up in policing his activities that I was barely able to do my job. The Allower in me didn't want to acknowledge that the relationship was over, and it was going to be over no matter what I did.

I'm sad to say that this wasn't the only time I used this tactic. Nor was it the only time it blew up in my face.

Recognizing this compulsive behavior of hanging on helped me see that I was replaying a piece of this pattern in my marriage. I needed to take a different path to prioritize my needs, and allow myself to communicate in a clear, concise way that wasn't intended to manipulate a particular response out of him. I needed to know my real value in the relationship, and stop seeing myself as a scorned woman. Once I made this shift, I could operate from a place of strength, regardless of what happened as the relationship drew to a close.

And so, as we moved toward divorce proceedings, I realized that there was nothing more for me to do. There was no guilt, no emotional hiccups. I wholeheartedly trusted my knowing that the marriage was over.

To have faith in a decision of that magnitude took a level of self-esteem and self-love I had never been able to summon before. I'll admit, there were a few moments where fear tried to creep in—but this time, I didn't grasp at straws. Instead, I looked to my future, and saw myself stepping into a new story as the extraordinary and resilient woman I am.

It's time now for you to take that step forward. You've looked back and seen your path clearly in the light of your broken heart. Now, it's time to climb out of the darkness and choose a new life, and a new way of loving.

SELF-REALIZATION QUESTIONS

- What do you feel is your Love Personality and why?

- What do you want to change about your Love Personality going forward?

- Is there someone (or many people) you need to forgive in order to leave this final part of your old love story behind?

- As you move into the work of writing a new love story for yourself, who do you want to be? What positive qualities do you want to embody?

CHAPTER EIGHT

BALANCE IS AN INTERNAL STATE

CHAPTER EIGHT

BALANCE IS AN INTERNAL STATE

"We are given two wines to drink in life, the white wine
of joy and the red wine of suffering. Until we have drunk
deeply of both, we have not lived fully."
- *Mechthild of Magdeburg*

I remember a morning, after my discovery of my husband's betrayal but before I made my final decision to divorce, when my husband came out of his office to join me on the couch, where I'd been meditating.

"Will you give me a Oneness blessing?" he asked.

We had actually done the training around this together as part of our attempt to reconcile our marriage. I was happy to perform the blessing. He seemed to really appreciate it.

After he left for work, I went down to his office and turned on his computer. Being a techno queen, it took me about ten seconds to figure out what he'd been doing before he asked me for that blessing. He'd been looking at porn.

I left the image up on his screen so that when he came home that night he would see it.

Of course, the first thing he did was make a beeline for his office. A few minutes later, he came back upstairs, looking sheepish. "I guess you saw that," he said. Like, *Aw, shucks!*

"You bet I did. I guess that was why you needed a blessing."

I was so conflicted that he'd try to pull that over on me. His intention to deceive me set alarm bells off through my entire body. What he'd been looking at wasn't as heart-rending or offensive as what I'd found that first day, but that hardly mattered. He knew how I felt, and he kept going back to it anyway.

"There's nothing to worry about," my husband said, looking deeply into my eyes. "Everything is okay. I was just clearing some old files."

I backed down in the moment, like I always did, and we went back to our evening almost as though nothing had happened. But I knew. My body knew. There was more to this than what I was allowing myself to see. It was time to do some deep digging.

Over the course of the next forty-eight hours, my world was shattered all over again.

I went back through my journals from the past few years, curious to know how many times I had backed down, how many times he had made promises that were empty and meaningless. Turns out, we'd had dozens of confrontations about the files that were still on his computer. Each time, he would look me in the eyes and vow that all of it would be deleted, that he would talk to someone, that there was nothing to worry about. However, a few days later, I'd find traces on his computer.

The worst was when he tried to access his computer remotely while traveling in California, and I happened to be in front of it at the time. I could see him trying to get into one of his special backup drives. I called him and said, "You know I can see what you're doing, right?"

When he came home, he drilled holes in all of his backup hard drives to "prove" that the files were gone. Of course, he'd already transferred them to a cloud server.

How had I let *that* one slide?

Poring over my journals, I was exhausted from all of the dishonesty. I couldn't believe that one person could tell so many lies. I was at the point where I didn't believe anything that came out of his mouth. His emotional pleas for me to believe him fell on deaf ears.

But what shattered me this time wasn't what he had done; it was what *I* had done. I had let fear rule me. I had ignored the warnings of my body, mind, and heart. Even now, I was avoiding the truth—skirting it, making excuses for him in my head. Why? Because I was afraid to admit that I'd done it again. I'd fallen for a man who didn't value me, and I'd stuck around to be walked on like a doormat over and over again.

Seeing the evidence spread out before me in my journals gave me the courage to finally face the truth. There was no other option for me but divorce. I could no longer make choices based on the historical patterns of this marriage, but in no other scenario would his lies remain acceptable. If I stayed, I would be doing so because I was wounded, afraid, and small.

Fully experiencing the dysfunction of what I'd been living broke my heart open even wider, but it also made my choice easy. Despite how scary it was to contemplate being alone at my age, or stepping out of the ashes of another failed relationship, or explaining to people what had really happened behind our closed doors, there was no other alternative for me than to leave.

I continued to work with this for several more weeks. Every morning, I would sit and write for an hour in my (well-hidden) journal. I recognized hundreds of moments in my marriage where I dismissed hurtful or disrespectful comments, or held myself back from sharing what I really felt. My life was so out of balance—and yet, I'd been pretending for our friends and family that everything was fine. I had abandoned myself in the relationship to keep the peace. I no longer had the desire to keep up this pretense. I was down to my bare bones; it was time to pull off all the masks and do whatever it took to get my internal equilibrium back.

It was time to put myself first, and reclaim my self-worth and self-respect. If *I* didn't stand up for me, he sure as hell wasn't going to.

I made a promise to myself. Looking into my own eyes in the bathroom mirror, I said, "Mal, you are *never* going to feel like this again. Ever."

And, unlike some people, I keep my promises.

For the first time in a long time, I could take a deep, cleansing breath all the way down into my belly, and not feel like I was choking. It was such a great feeling that I laughed out loud.

RECLAIMING INNER *Balance*

After you've shed the last dead weight of your old love story, it's time to find inner balance again. The more honest you can be with yourself at this point, the more quickly you will restore your emotional equilibrium. Inner balance will bring closure; it will eradicate any remaining feelings of victimhood. It will give you level ground to stand on as you contemplate your first steps forward into your new life.

The first thing to notice is how you feel in your body. When you are out of balance, your body will immediately start to send you warning signs. Fear, in particular, has a feeling. Whenever you are acting out of fear, your body will shrink. You will literally get smaller. You'll try to take up less space. You'll breathe shallowly.

Start to notice when you are in fear. When you are, write about it. What do you fear? What are you avoiding? What will happen if you do what's best for you, instead of simply doing what you've always done?

Sometimes, the answers aren't clear. To help me make better decisions, I started using this practice to draw the truth from my wounded heart. Draw two columns in your journal. Label one "What do I fear?" and the other "How can I balance this fear?" It's a variation on the old "problems/solutions" list.

On the next page, I've created a chart as an example. Feel free to copy it in your journal whenever your fear threatens to get the best of you.

What do I fear?	How can I balance this fear?
Not speaking up	Declare my needs Decide what I will not accept
No emotional support	Get professional help Make more time for spiritual practice
Other people's judgment	Spend more time with supportive friends
Being single at my age	Meet new people every week
Loneliness	Join a support group Educate myself on the topic

When you do this, not only will you start to recognize the historical fears related to your old love story, but the cultural and inherited fears we discussed in Chapter Seven that are still hanging on in the background. You will also see your strengths, your weaknesses, and how you are accustomed to treating yourself.

Let's face it: heartbreak is a significant physiological and psychological injury. But just like with any injury, once the wounds are scabbed over, you need to start moving again. You need to get your balance back, and strengthen the weak muscles, even when you'd rather just lie there in bed. Otherwise, you'll be limping for the rest of your life.

I assign this practice of morning writing and fear/solution identification to my coaching clients who are going through relationship traumas. They write every morning, pouring themselves onto the paper, letting all of the shadows slink across the pages. They let all of the anger, all of the terror, and all of the jealousy rip. They release their pent-up emotions so they can start to breathe again. And when the practice is done, they feel more balanced. More clear. More stable. All of them, one hundred percent of the time.

OTHER *Tools* FOR BALANCE

There are other tools I use for balancing my inner state that can be done at any time. Conscious breathing has been miraculous for me, and for my clients, in terms of calming the body and restoring balance.

In yogic practice, conscious breathing is called *prāṇāyāma*, which loosely translates as "breath control." One of the easiest practices of *prāṇāyāma* is called *nadi shodhana*, or "alternate nostril breathing." This balances the energy inside your body and helps calm your nervous system.

To do this exercise, place your right thumb on the right side of your nose. Curl your index and middle fingers into your palm, and place your right ring finger and pinky on the left side of your nose. Now, use your thumb to close your right nostril, and inhale through the left nostril. When you are full, hold the breath while you release the right nostril and close the left with your ring finger and pinky. Then, exhale through your right nostril.

On the next round, inhale through the right nostril, then exhale through the left. Repeat this at least ten times. I promise, you will feel like a whole new person when you're done!

Another quick and easy breathing exercise that you can do anywhere is to simply inhale for a count of four, hold the breath for a count of two, and exhale for a count of six. This slows the breath way down and forces you to inhale more deeply.

121

It's natural to shut down after heartbreak. In fact, it's an automatic way to protect ourselves from further injury. We surround ourselves with thoughts of avoiding, armoring, and defending—and it feels temporarily strong and comforting to be in that place. But soon, you'll realize that when you're locked up tight inside your fortress, no one can get in ... but you can't get out, either.

More, when you're armored up or twisted into a knot like a pretzel, it's pretty hard to breathe. In fact, it's hard to do anything that matters. Your breath is the lifeline that connects you to your inner power and sense of well-being. Each time you take a conscious breath, you take a small step to reconnecting with your wholeness, self-worth, and self-love.

It's painful to see how many women choose to stay broken and helpless—or armored and angry—for years after a betrayal. Believe me, you don't want to choose that. But you don't have to let it go all at once, either. Instead, start to recognize when you get that "tight" feeling inside, and combat it with breath. When you do, you'll immediately start to see solutions that weren't available to you before.

Balance comes one step at a time—like when you're walking on a tightrope, or a balance beam. You just put one foot in front of the other, and do what needs to be done to stay level in each moment. And, like anything else, it takes practice.

Take a step, girl. You can do it.

122 SELF-REALIZATION QUESTIONS

- How does it feel to start creating solutions to your fears?

- What promise will you make to yourself today?

- What actions are you consciously choosing to help you feel better right now?

- Can you find time throughout your day today (and every day) to pause and take a deep breath?

CHAPTER NINE

YOU ARE THE LOVE YOU NEED

CHAPTER NINE

YOU ARE THE LOVE YOU NEED

"The expression 'I am worthy of my own love despite this hardship' is the seed that brings light into the darkest moments of our lives." - *Miguel Ruiz*

*H*ave you ever been at a party, and notice that the room just … stops for a moment?

You turn, and see why everyone is staring. An attractive woman just walked in. All heads have turned toward her. She smiles, and the room smiles back.

You notice something compelling about her, but you can't pinpoint it. She's not a supermodel, or a celebrity. It's not the hair, or the dress, or the shoes. It's *her*.

You ask yourself, "What does she have that I don't?"

She exudes confidence and worthiness. She's not making a scene or a bold entry, but rather a very comfortable one. The more you look at her, the more you feel that there's a *lightness* emanating from her. You want to know her. You want to become her.

You want what she has.

And you can have it. We all can. Girl, that woman isn't special, or better than you. She wasn't born with magical powers. She's simply wrapped in a cloak of self-love!

There is nothing more complimentary to a woman than real self-love. Women who love themselves stand out in a crowd. They *shine.* They aren't defined by what other people think, or by the men who stand next to them. They're enough on their own.

You can have this kind of confidence. In fact, it's one of the great gifts of being broken open—*if* you're willing to clear the way to receive it.

THE *Truth* IN THE MIRROR

When was the last time you looked in a mirror and said to yourself, "You are precious and important! You are worthy of love, connection, and living with purpose!"?

Probably not in a long time. But it's not too late to start living like a woman who owns her worth.

Take a deep breath. Step in front of that mirror and say to yourself, "I am worthy of happiness in my life. I am not afraid to be seen. I know how to love greatly, because I have loved before, even when it hurt me. Now, I will love *me* more than I've ever loved anyone else."

You are so much more than the hot mess you've just gone through. All the love you need is already within you. You just have to let it out of the cage you've built for it.

Our old love stories would have us believe that we needed

to wait for a Prince Charming to ride in on his steed to rescue us and "give" us the love we craved—to unlock our hearts and set us free. We know now that this is victim thinking. Instead, we need to rescue ourselves.

If you have done the practices I have suggested in previous chapters, you are on a path of healing. When you add in a consistent spiritual (not narcissistic or egotistical) practice of loving yourself, you will have everything you need to heal your wounded heart. You will have tapped into the infinite well of love within you.

This love has been inside you all along. You never again need to chase after it with short skirts, push-up bras, or stilettos. You never again need to sacrifice your integrity on the altar of someone else's lies to keep it. You never again need to put up with bullshit or abuse to "earn" it. You never again need to doubt that you are worthy of it.

WHO DO YOU *See?*

For the next several weeks, I want you to do this mirror exercise every morning, just before your journaling practice.

Look deeply into your own eyes. Tell that beautiful woman in the mirror just how much you love her, and how committed you are to her happiness. Tell her that you cherish her, and will protect her. Create your own affirmations to reinforce your belief in your beauty, prosperity, worthiness, bravery, and divine right to be loved. Say it like you mean it.

As you speak to yourself and stare into your own eyes, do a little self-massage with scented oils or lotion. Gently caress your face, your arms, your belly and legs and breasts with long, smooth strokes while you speak your loving words. Show appreciation for the magnificent temple that holds your heart. Be with yourself.

At first, this will feel awkward and uncomfortable. Don't stop doing it! Like anything else, this will get easier with practice. You will make breakthroughs. Walls will come down. Each time, you'll let more light in.

MORE WAYS TO *love* YOURSELF

Sometimes, we don't even realize the ways in which we are withholding love from ourselves. But if we want to tap into that latent power, we need to become conscious of all the little things that build us up or break us down, every day.

First, become conscious of what you're reading, watching on TV, or watching online. How do you feel in your body while you're consuming this "entertainment"? For example, if you're already nervous about living alone for the first time in twenty-five years, murder mysteries aren't going to help you feel safe and calm! It sounds silly, but the more you observe how certain things make you feel in your body, the more you'll want to "clean up" what you're taking in on a sensory level.

Next, read! Find some spiritual teachers and books that speak to your soul. You can find a helpful list at the back of this book, as well as on my website. I have found that when I need comfort, the best thing for me to do is to turn to my spiritual teachers.

Play music that lights you on fire. Dance around your

house—naked if you like—and let yourself move like a wild woman. This isn't just fun. It actually activates the life force within you, and helps you feel deeply at home in your body.

Look at the food that you are putting into your temple. Is it healthy? Will it nourish your beautiful body? Are you consuming too much sugar, flour, or other irritants? If you're not getting enough vitamins and minerals in your food, be sure to include good-quality supplements. As you learn to love yourself, you will also learn to give your body what it truly wants and needs, not what gives you momentary satisfaction.

When you truly love yourself, it will be apparent in your skin, hair, body, and energy. You will recognize what is in alignment for you, and make your choices from that place. It may sound simple, but usually what feels good is right for you. When something causes you agitation, doubt, fear, or uncertainty, that's a signal that you're walking down the wrong path. When you feel crystal clear, it usually means you're in alignment with your soul, your higher self, and the love within you.

When you consistently practice loving yourself, you will gain confidence. You will be able to set aside the inner conflicts pulling you in multiple directions, and just go with what your soul is asking for. You will be standing on solid ground.

You can replicate that clarity over and over by just slowing the heck down. Most of our choices every day are made by default. They're automatic, habitual. So, while you're forming new, self-loving habits, it's important to assess everything. Every time you make a choice—about food, an activity, media, or anything else—take a deep breath before you leap. Ask yourself, "Is this really what I want and need right now? Will it help me get where I want to go?"

If you don't know the answer, don't take action until you figure it out. Writing things out in your journal is helpful. The process of writing will allow things to flow more freely by getting you out of your head; then, more possibilities will bubble up.

Most importantly, don't judge anything you do, say, think, or feel right now. It's too early to dismiss options. Instead, be willing to try everything. Not everything will work, but your inner wisdom will help you discern what to keep and what to leave behind.

When you allow yourself to grow into your self-love and inner wisdom, something magical will happen. Other people's opinions and beliefs will cease to matter so much to you. You'll have a deeper understanding that we are all on our own paths, and each of us is unique. You will decide how your story is told.

AN INNER *Rebirth*

When you awaken love within yourself, it's a rebirth to a new you. It's a new beginning. You will feel a sense of fulfillment and wholeness you may never have experienced before, even when you were in a relationship.

When I started my research for this book, I spoke to so many women who admitted that they were holding on to someone they no longer wanted to be with. They knew it probably was not a good match, but it was better than having no one.

I totally got it. As I've shared with you, I did the same thing. I ignored my intuition, my body's signals, and the evidence of my own eyes—all to keep together a relationship that wasn't working. Each time I brushed off something inexcusable, I cut myself off from self-love.

One of the most challenging circumstances we can be in as women is to know that where we are isn't working, but also that we're too afraid to change the situation. This is comparable to dying a slow death. Your self-worth slowly rots away over time. The impact that is caused mentally and physically is rarely worth it.

Sadly, it often takes a catastrophe—like a betrayal, or something equally as devastating—to wake us up to this slow erosion.

For example, I worked with a lovely girl named Sarah, who had recently been diagnosed with breast cancer. For years prior to her diagnosis, she was miserable in her marriage. Daily, she wondered how she would get through the rest of her life like this. And yet, she resisted making a change until that awful day when she felt a lump in her breast.

There were no words to describe the sheer panic that ran through every cell in her body when she got the test results. She was down to life or death.

"It was a massive wake-up call," she told me. "But if I was going to have to fight to survive, I was going to make damned sure I was happy when it was all done!"

Mere weeks after starting treatment, she told her husband that she was leaving.

It took a cancer diagnosis for Sarah to decide that she was worthy of happiness, and that her own joy was something worth fighting for. For me, it took a betrayal. It's a tough way to realize the value of your life.

133

You don't have to wait for another crisis to start to appreciate what you have, and start to prioritize your self-love, happiness, and well-being. You don't have to wait until you're completely

alone to learn to love your own company. You don't have to wait until a life-or-death crossroads to make the choice to heal. You don't have to wait until all of your choices have been taken away to give yourself permission to ask for what you want.

You are co-creating with the Universe at all times to manifest your heart's desires. Loving yourself means loving the greatest force that exists, because you are inseparable from it. The love within you can create miracles, but only if you clear the way first.

Self-love gives you the opportunity to make all the wrongs in your life right. None of us grew up in perfect families with perfect lives and no suffering. Every one of us has made mistakes. And yet, we carry our sorrows with us for years, sometimes lifetimes. Self-love can wipe away many of those judgments. Self-love will never let you down; it can only build you up.

With self-love also comes self-knowledge. You can no longer be ignorant of the reasons why you do what you do—but you don't have to judge them, either. And, because you have this understanding, you can also be more compassionate and caring toward others.

Spiritual texts in all philosophies write about the lesson of self-love. It is the most important lesson you will ever learn. Nothing will change your life faster or more radically than you loving yourself. Nothing will change the quality of your relationships with others more than self-love. Self-love can create heaven on earth for you. But if you refuse it, you will make your life a living hell.

There are four key steps to establishing self-love:

- *Practice mindfulness.* Be aware of how you feel about yourself in any given situation. Be present with your feelings; don't ignore them.

- *Take care of yourself and your health—mental and physical.* Make yourself a priority in your life. If you don't, no one else will.

- *Create healthy boundaries in all of your relationships.* When you feel respected by others, and ask for that respect through boundaries, you will build self-worth.

- *Forgive yourself and others.* Forgiveness frees us from the pain we're carrying. More, it cuts the cords tying you to your old, painful love story.

A favorite quote of mine by Ralph Waldo Emerson reads, "What lies behind us and what lies before us are small matters compared to what lies within us."

The quality of your life moving forward will be in direct proportion to the love you have for yourself. When you make the choice to love yourself completely, write yourself a love poem—a prayer for all that you desire. Put into it all that your heart is yearning for.

On the next page is a prayer that I wrote for myself a few months ago: This is a perfect example of what can come out of you when you allow love to move through you.

REALIZATION

Where there were once fragments

There is now wholeness

Where there was once darkness and stabbing unworthiness

There is now love and light

Where there was a young woman's heart filled with fear

There is now peace and contentment

Where the words "I AM" once frightened me

The words now uplift me

Where there was once a desire for death

There is now a deep love for living

The pieces all fit beautifully into the mosaic of a divine feminine soul

What a mystical journey from desperation to transformation

For the first time I am home—complete within myself

I AM a child of God filled with divine light, here to bring love and courage to others.

You can be that woman who lights up a room. That kind of presence, light, and power is only ever a breath away.

SELF-REALIZATION QUESTIONS

- On a scale of one to ten, how much do you truly love yourself?

- What fears do you have around stepping into self-love?

- What have you observed about the way you treat yourself and how that reflects your level of self-love?

- What old judgments or ideas do you need to let go of so that you can be more loving to yourself?

- What would it feel like to take one self-loving action per day, every day?

- What would it take for you to step into unapologetic self-love right now?

CHAPTER TEN

WE ARE RESPONSIBLE FOR EVERYTHING

CHAPTER TEN

WE ARE RESPONSIBLE FOR EVERYTHING

"Unless we look with the eyes of love, we cannot see things as they are." - *Kabir Helminski*

*M*y friend Janet married a man she didn't love.

She was in her early forties, and had been dreaming of a man who loved to travel, hike, go to concerts, and spend time on the water, just like she did. But Mister Right wasn't showing his face.

Jim had been pursuing her for a while. He was a good-natured bank manager with a dry sense of humor and a penchant for mystery novels. He also had a huge fear of flying, got violently seasick, and hated both crowds and loud music.

"He's not my Prince Charming," Janet told me once. "But he's a good guy, and he's stable, and he loves me. I guess that's enough to go on. Maybe we'll grow into each other." She was afraid that if she didn't get hitched soon, she would be alone forever.

Unsurprisingly, this was a perfect setup for heartbreak and disappointment.

Janet didn't feel empowered in her marriage. She tried to be a "good wife," but she felt like a dependent instead of an equal partner. She hadn't magically fallen in love with her hubby over the past seven years; in fact, everything he did seemed to get on her nerves. She kept wondering if she should leave—but now she was nearing fifty, and being single again was too frightening to contemplate.

When Janet's husband asked her, out of the blue, for a divorce, I can't say I was surprised. Nor was she, really. But the betrayal of his abandonment hit her in her core. She'd tried to do everything "right," and she'd still gotten screwed over.

Janet immediately defaulted to blaming her husband for deserting her, disregarding her feelings, and turning her life upside down. But after a while, she began to remember the vision of her ideal man—the one she'd never really let go. She realized that she was, in large part, responsible for creating her loveless marriage. In fact, Jim had tried far harder than she had to make it work for years.

I asked her, "What if this is your chance to get what you really wanted all along?"

She smiled. "You know what? Maybe it is!"

LIFE HAPPENS *Through* YOU, NOT *To* YOU

Here's a question for you: Are you willing, right here and now, to embrace the concept that everything happens *through* us and not *to* us?

The struggles that appear in our lives are meant to be teaching tools, taking us to a higher level of self-awareness. Every relationship you engage in serves a purpose. Through these engagements, you can choose to heal the past, release the old perceptions, and rewire yourself emotionally. You can choose to emerge from each new phase of your life like a lotus growing out of the mud—or you can burrow deeper into the shit. It's up to you.

Every relationship, regardless of how it begins or ends, is a messenger to your heart. You can choose to listen to it, or ignore it. This *is* a choice, even if you weren't aware of it until now.

So many women create identities based on their relationships. You know that I did it—and I know I'm not alone. But a woman with a healthy sense of self knows how to negotiate the tricky waters of intimacy without selling her soul.

The way to do this is as plain as the nose on your face. It's just that no one has ever taught you how—until now.

The truth is, nothing is random. In some way, you have (knowingly or unknowingly) radiated an energy that attracted certain people into your life in certain ways. We've already talked in depth about how your love story creates your love life, so I won't rehash that here—but I will add to it with some information that may be new to you.

It has been said by many spiritual teachers that you actually choose the family that you are born into, and the people who will be key players in your life. If you can wrap your mind around that, it's a huge paradigm shift. It means that everything that has happened to you—every sad scene in your love story, every bump in your road—happened as an integral part of your soul's development. When you fully embrace the fact that there is a larger plan in play, it eliminates much of the resistance you may feel, so you can tip the scales in your favor for real happiness.

Your fear is as great a teacher as your heartbreak. When you learn to trust yourself and your decisions—through your journaling, your self-inquiry process, and getting connected to your body and breath—you can begin to push that fear out of your body. Remember, your fear is always tied to your pride, your vanity, your ego, or your survival instincts in some way. Love is connected to your heart, and it never asks you to compromise on your values or your dignity.

So, it's truth time: Now that you understand how your fears, your love story, and your choices have contributed to creating the experience that broke you open, and are open to the possibility that all of this was divinely orchestrated as a profound learning experience for your greatest benefit … do you have a different appreciation for your part in it?

When I ask women this question in a class I teach, I get a similar response from many of the women. Upon reflection, their love story and actions in the relationship did, in fact, contribute to the outcome. And once they agreed to learn from what had happened, and did the work to heal their love stories so as not to repeat the same mistakes, they gained a whole new appreciation for themselves, their lives, and their power as awakened women.

My client Suzanne is a perfect example of this. She was noticing a progression of odd behavior on the part of her husband. He started running late more frequently. He started working longer hours. He didn't bring his laptop in from the car at night, or leave his cell phone on the hallway table. Sometimes when he came home, he jumped right into the shower without even saying hello to her or the kids. He seemed preoccupied, and less physically interested in her.

However, she didn't act on any of her observations. Already stressed by the demands of career, kids, and household, she refused to look at the warning signs that there was trouble in her marriage. She just kept her head down and hoped it would all work itself out.

Several months later, nothing had changed. In fact, her husband's behavior had gone from strange to downright sneaky. Finally she couldn't stand it any longer. While he was in the shower, she tiptoed upstairs to the bedroom and slipped his phone out of the pocket of his jacket. He'd changed the code, but she guessed it quickly enough.

The first thing she saw was a green text message alert on the home screen. When she read the text, she crumpled to the ground. It was like a knife had stabbed her in the heart.

Her husband was involved with another woman. From the text thread, she guessed they had been an item for a while. Suddenly, all the little oddities she'd ignored came crashing back into her mind as warning signs.

He came out of the bathroom to find her sobbing on the floor. He didn't try to hide anything. "I've been meaning to tell you for a while," he said. "It just never seemed like the right time. But the fact is, I'm leaving."

Suzanne's mind raced. Maybe if she had intervened earlier, if she had paid attention to his odd behavior instead of burying her head in the sand, she would still have a marriage. But rather than have a difficult conversation, she chose to ignore what was happening.

"This is all my fault," she whispered. "I did this to us."

When we connected, Suzanne was filled with guilt. She was still blaming herself for her husband's affair.

145

"Honey, his decisions are not your fault," I told her. "Even if you found out earlier, you might not have been able to change the trajectory of the marriage. But what you *can* own is your own unwillingness to have a hard conversation, and follow through on your gut feelings. It was your choice to ignore that knot in your stomach. But the rest? That's not on you."

Suzanne is not the only woman I know who hesitated to ask difficult questions in order to avoid confrontation. Fannie, too, ignored her intuition—but the man who broke her heart wasn't her husband. He was someone else's.

She knew he was too good to be true. Romantic weekend getaways, lavish hotel suites, and fancy restaurants were normal in their relationship. Her nickname for him, amongst her friends, was "The Duke." He had a penthouse apartment in the city, but they rarely stayed there, and he wouldn't give her a key. There were whole weeks when he didn't return her calls. He said he was away on business, but come to find out, he was at home in a lavish suburb with his wife and kids.

He never came out and admitted that he was married and a father. She actually found out about his marriage because he'd won a prestigious award at his company, and she'd Googled the press release. When she saw a picture of him standing next to a lovely blond woman, her heart hit the floor. "A dedicated husband and father of four …" the caption read.

Fannie had known something wasn't adding up. But she wanted so much to believe in her Prince Charming that she brushed off his unwillingness to let her into his personal space. In hindsight, of course, she saw it clearly. Now, she was carrying not only the hurt of a broken heart, but also the guilt of being the "other woman," however ignorant she'd been.

When we start to take responsibility for our part in our

broken hearts, the first step is to acknowledge that it is always our choice to respect or ignore our deepest desires, intuition, and inner knowing. As we've discussed, I ignored red flags the size of Mount Everest, all in the name of preserving the relationship. If I had listened to my gut, I would have found out about his betrayal a lot sooner, and saved myself a lot of grief. However, in my naïve desire to avoid conflict (or, even worse, prove myself right and have to live with the consequences) I allowed the situation to get completely out of hand.

All my life, I've stuffed what I was actually feeling in a closet so that I could avoid confrontation and keep my relationships going. The choices I thought would give me more control ultimately robbed me of my power.

Once I admitted that, and owned it, two things happened. First, I experienced a huge sense of relief. Never again would I follow this subconscious pattern into a broken heart; it was out in the open, ready to be healed. Second, I felt empowered, because now I had the knowledge and capability to make better choices.

Now that you've unraveled your love story and some of the "why" of your broken heart, it's time to reflect on where your choices to compromise yourself, ignore your intuition, and stuff away your feelings may have allowed, inflamed, or compounded the situation. Again, I'm not asking you to take responsibility for the actions of the one who betrayed you: that's on them. But I *am* asking you to own your own contribution to the dynamic.

Self-reflection is the greatest tool you have at your disposal, now and always. You need to keep asking those tough questions, like "Why did I pick him? What did I expect to get out of this relationship? What did I contribute to the overall dynamic?

147

Where did my actions cause harm to me or to him? Where was I wrapped up in fear, and where was I empowered?" Write out your answers to those questions, and any others that come into your mind. Soon, you'll start to see where your responsibilities lie, and where they most definitely do not.

You've come to a crossroads of understanding. You've learned so much already. But in order to *heal*, you must *feel*—and taking responsibility for what you've created is a big part of that, especially if your avoidance patterns were part of the issue in the first place.

Thankfully, neither Suzanne nor Fannie feel like victims anymore. They have left their old relationships behind, owned their parts in what happened, and done the inner work to heal their old love stories. Fannie even took the step of writing a letter of apology to her ex's wife, owning fully her own part in the affair, regardless of the fact that she didn't know he was married. She never sent the letter (she burned it instead) but after writing it she felt more empowered than ever before in her life.

Taking full responsibility will do that to you. It takes a lot of courage to stand up and say, "Something is wrong. I'll own my part and do what I can to repair it." Where once you felt like a victim, you now feel like a warrior for real love.

WHAT DO YOU *Think* YOU DESERVE?

The time has come for women to speak their truth, and that includes you. Being more proactive in addressing your needs saves you from painful overreacting down the road. You were given a gift of intuition to formulate important choices. It's like putting all the pieces of a puzzle together so you can see a picture.

One of my favorite teachers, Louise Hay, once said, "All relationships are mirrors of ourselves." Now, doesn't *that* inspire some deep reflection?

It's simple, but profound at the same time. So many of our relationships play out in painful ways because, at a core level, we don't feel worthy. When we don't value and respect ourselves, we can project that feeling to a partner. That person responds to our vibration of "not worthy" by treating us like we're not worthy.

None of us consciously want to attract someone who will inflict emotional or bodily harm. You might not even be aware that your core beliefs are bringing predators into your energy field. But if you constantly feel walked on, disregarded, or ignored, or if you're being abused in any way, it's important to realize that how you feel about yourself is contributing to that dynamic. That doesn't excuse your abusers, or those who take advantage of you—but how you feel about yourself is totally within your control. When you learn to love and respect yourself, you won't attract—or stand for—those kinds of behaviors anymore.

If you just take this one lesson and work with it wholeheartedly, the quality of your life will change significantly.

I know today that every abusive situation I got myself into when I was younger was a result of how poorly I felt about me. I would socialize with men who preyed on women like me. They knew they could manipulate a weak woman, and they did it over and over. If I had any self-esteem, I probably would never have set foot in the same room with them—but sadly, I didn't. I lacked the courage to speak up to them or to cry out to someone else for help. Subconsciously, I thought I was getting what I deserved.

Sadly, as long as there are women who don't respect themselves, there will be jerks that prey on them. I want to put an end to women being abused because of how they feel about themselves. I want to teach them to love themselves so that they can be loved and respected in relationships.

Owning up to your self-esteem issues may be the hardest thing you ever do. Speaking this truth out loud for the first time was one of the hardest things I've ever done. But once the words were out, and the tears were shed, I felt like a whole new woman. Although I'd lost nearly everything, I still had *me*. And the woman I found myself to be was brave enough to be vulnerable, trustworthy enough to own her shit, and determined enough not to let a broken heart be the end of her story. In so many ways, she was proving to be stronger and more resilient than I could have ever imagined.

You will need to look deeply within yourself to decipher the answers, and the areas where you've been avoiding responsibility. But when you do, every single upset that you have experienced will take on a new flavor and meaning.

Everything has purpose. It's our job to figure out what that purpose is—to see the lesson that's being presented as a match to ignite our personal transformation. It's not always about adversity; it's more about educating and birthing the divine woman you already are inside.

When you heal low self-esteem and recognize your worth, it is a major step forward in healing your heart. When you know you deserve to be happy, it's hard to settle for anything less.

SELF-REALIZATION QUESTIONS

- Have you ignored your intuition, been complacent, or shied away from expressing your truth?

- What dynamic did that behavior create?

- What part of your broken heart are you truly responsible for? How can you own this without guilt or shame?

- What parts of your broken heart are you absolutely not responsible for?

- Do you feel worthy in your life? Why or why not?

- What is one thing you can do right now to bolster your self-worth and self-trust?

The best thing about taking responsibility for your role in your past relationships is that it allows you to say—and mean—those magical words: "I'll never do *that* again!"

Once again, in order to heal, you must feel. You can extinguish the inner fires that fuel conflict, grief, anger—or, in my case, addiction. Recognizing how you have battled your own thoughts and feelings ends the internal war; by taking charge of your own inner battlefield, you can come to an amazing state of peace within yourself.

Embracing complete and unequivocal responsibility for my thoughts, actions, and choices stopped the war within me. I came off the battlefield a glorious, self-loving warrior. I was no longer undermining my intuition. I trusted my decisions because I was no longer conflicted. And I could seek the help

I needed to grow and heal because I wasn't hiding from my own choices anymore. I faced my fears and I regained my confidence. For the first time in my life, I am free from the screeching dialogue of a condemning inner critic.

You can't keep doing the same thing over and over and expect to create different results. That's the definition of insanity. Taking responsibility isn't just about reclaiming your power; it's literally about self-preservation. You *deserve* to be happy, and settling for behavior that erodes your self-worth, undermines your security, and keeps you locked in insecurity can cause deep emotional and physical repercussions—even if the person you're settling for that behavior from is *you*. Getting out of a bad situation can only lead you to creating new possibilities in the future. When you move your mind from damage control to creating what you want, life starts to look very different.

You get to control three things for sure in your life: your thoughts, your feelings, and your choices. Happiness is your birthright, but you still need to claim it.

Let's start learning how.

CHAPTER ELEVEN

FREEDOM IS FORGIVENESS

CHAPTER ELEVEN

FREEDOM IS FORGIVENESS

"Forgiveness is giving up all hope for a better past." -
Gerald Jampolsky

This past year, I worked with a group of women in recovery. Two of the twelve women had been sexually abused as children by a family member.

One, who we'll call Tanya, had been molested by her uncle as a small child. Whenever he came to the house, they would sit together under a blanket while they were watching television. He was able to put his hands in her pants in the middle of the living room, amongst family, with no one the wiser.

The second woman, Stephanie, had been raped by her stepfather. Although she tried to alert her mother to what was happening, her mother refused to believe her. It went on for a long while before the authorities got involved.

Both situations were deep and horrific betrayals of young women. What was so unusual was the radically different life paths they chose after the abuse.

Tanya became a heroin addict and was consumed with anger and shame. She was never able to get into long term recovery because every time she got clean the pain kept flooding back. She lived as a helpless victim to her circumstances and her addiction. Stephanie, on the other hand, while she also spiraled into addiction for several years, eventually chose to forgive her stepfather so that she could move forward with her life.

I spent several hours speaking with Stephanie privately to understand how she picked up the pieces of her shattered life.

My eyes filled with tears as Stephanie told me how her own mother had rejected her after the rape. She couldn't bring herself to believe that this man whom she loved, and had recently married, was sneaking into her daughter's bedroom at night and abusing her. At fourteen years old, Stephanie was still very much a child, although her well-developed body made her seem older. She believed her stepfather when he threatened to hurt her mother if Stephanie didn't keep quiet. She believed him when he said that he would call the authorities and put her and her brother in a home for "delinquent children" if she didn't comply.

Stephanie eventually ran away. She tried to survive on the streets, but was eventually picked up for prostitution and drugs. She calls the day of her arrest "the luckiest day of my life" because she was ordered into a rehab program that started her recovery.

Extraordinarily smart and driven, Stephanie managed to graduate from high school while still in a detention facility. She was moved to a recovery home after demonstrating her exceptional commitment to getting well. She studied constantly, and was involved in various in-house programs to expedite her healing process. Eventually, she was led back to that horrible trauma which had originally broken her open.

Stephanie started writing letters to her stepfather. Each was more painful than the last. She described in detail how her innocence was taken away, how she was forced to do things out of fear that her family would be punished. She kept asking herself, "What was in his heart when he was doing these terrible things? What happened to him to make him want to do this?"

She had a stack of black and white composition books filled with letters and deep journaling. Determined to come to peace with this part of her life, she refused to live in hatred of her stepfather. She knew that anger and shame would hold her hostage to what she had been through. She wanted a new life—a different life. And she created the vision for that life through her writing practice.

She trusted me to read some of her journals. I got choked up as I thumbed through the tear-splattered pages, and my heart broke as I read the graphic details of her violation. She didn't hold back, even in those first entries. But as time went on, the emotions on those pages changed as she realized that she was no longer threatened by this man who had broken her open.

When her mother and her stepfather (who was now incarcerated) came to her to ask her forgiveness, she chose to grant it. Not for them, but for herself. She wanted to be free, and forgiveness was her path to freedom. She forgave them for what they had done, and herself for thinking that she had somehow caused it. She rewrote her story, and used it as the basis for a brand new life.

Soon, Stephanie was helping other women who came into the rehab facility after similar experiences. She wanted to be a powerful example for them. Soon, she came to feel that her trauma had not broken her, but had instead empowered her to do more good with her life than she had ever imagined possible.

ARE YOU READY TO *Forgive?*

You've come a long way, girl.

You've learned so much about yourself. You've delved into your love story. You've explored your fears, and your mistakes, and you've taken full responsibility for all of your shit. You probably have a whole new perspective on your broken heart.

But are you willing to forgive the one who cracked you open? Are you willing to forgive yourself?

At this point, you have two choices: you can stay pissed off, in a self-righteous victim mentality reinforcing that you got royally screwed over … or you can pull yourself into the present moment and ask, "Do I really want to continue to feel this way?"

As Gandhi said, "The weak can never forgive. Forgiveness is the attribute of the strong."

If you've been betrayed, your angry feelings are justified. But you can't let them take over your life. There is nothing to be gained by belaboring your anger. Remember, your current reality is the result of your projections; you may not have chosen or created the situation, but now that it's over, you are *recreating* it with your angry thoughts. You keep wishing for a different outcome, but (unless you really have developed a time machine) there's no way to go back and change the past. What's done is done.

Forgiveness will restore your equilibrium. It is a personal act, one that you must consciously choose. When you've had enough of the pain, of feeling connected to past events, and of feeling unable to smile because of the weight of your baggage, it's time to cut those energetic cords and start moving forward again. Forgiveness doesn't erase the past, it only releases your emotional attachment to it so you can focus on the present, and your new future. You don't have to forget what happened, but it doesn't need to run your life anymore.

Your power only exists in the present. When you are stuck in the past, you have nothing.

When I decided I was ready to forgive my husband and let go of my broken heart, I began praying every day to Archangel Michael, whose sword cuts through the cords that keep us attached to past events and past lives. These cords were the nonstop running dialogue in my head about how much pain I was in, how awful my situation was, and how furious I was at him and myself. I asked that Michael cut any and all cords binding me to my husband—to bring them to light, and sever them with compassion. I closed each morning practice with a request for the highest and best outcome for both of us.

The funny thing is, forgiveness is subtle. It's almost anticlimactic. For a little while, you may feel like nothing is happening. But soon, you'll start to notice the full impact of the change you've made.

Pain is real, but suffering is a choice. You can't change another person, or the past, or your own mistakes. But you can accept what is, and move forward from exactly where you are. This is your chance to empty yourself of all the poison that's still swimming around in your heart and polluting your mind. You can finally let go of the hope that things could have been, or will someday be, different.

THE REAL *Price* OF ANGER

Anger is physically depleting, and it gets you nowhere. It might feel easier to stay angry and condemn the other person;

this requires no work on your part, no introspection, and no bravery. But in the long run, anger is a heavy burden to bear, and the person it hurts most will always be you.

Anger, hatred, and jealousy can take a terrible toll on your body. I'm sure you are aware that doctors now believe there is a direct link between mental and emotional stress levels and certain types of cancer, heart disease, and stroke. When you are constantly angry, your body perceives that there is a threat, and prepares itself accordingly. This creates chronic stress that can (literally and figuratively) steal your life away.

There isn't one single good reason to hang on to anger and deep unhappiness. It will rob you of your health, your joy, and your future. Women who are consumed with self-pity, who wallow in the past and in circumstances that no longer exist, are doing themselves more harm than they know. It takes a lot of work to create pain in the present when the event is in the past. All of that energy could be going toward something productive, instead of to constantly recreating and retelling an old, sad story.

I worked with a young woman named Jamie who had been divorced for over five years. Even after all that time, she still experienced rage and outright hatred toward her ex. She was also constantly challenged with health issues, including uterine and vaginal complications. She had issues at work with job performance and meeting deadlines. Truthfully, she was mentally consumed by her divorce and could barely focus on anything else. She couldn't let go of the fact that her husband had cheated on her, and ultimately left her.

That betrayal was all she talked about. She kept telling that story, over and over. One day, I stopped her as kindly as I could, and said, "Honey, if you ever want to have love and happiness again, you need to stop resisting what happened. It's time for you to create a new story."

Jamie burst into heavy sobs. I held her hand and reassured her that she was going to be okay. We walked slowly through the history of her relationship to see where she might have unconsciously initiated conflict with her husband. She realized she had a deeply-buried resentment because he was so attractive; women flirted with him, which made her feel panicky that he might one day flirt back. After an evening out with him, she would obsess for days, rethinking every detail to see if she had missed anything that would indicate infidelity.

Going through this, Jamie realized that she had manifested his leaving by her constant thinking that he would. She was stunned to realize that she had gotten exactly what she expected.

When she took responsibility for her part in creating the relationship, Jamie started to feel lighter. With a continued practice of forgiving herself and her ex, her physical ailments started to go away. She let go of the pain that she had kept buried in her body, reopened the energy flow, and reclaimed her power of choice and creative energy.

Several months after our first conversation, she actually initiated a call to her ex-husband. The conversation brought about much-needed closure and understanding for both of them.

"I was so fearful all the time," she told him. "That must have been so difficult for you. I never trusted you, not even in the beginning."

"I'm so sorry, too, Jamie," her ex replied. "It was never my intention for the affair to happen, and I never meant to hurt you so badly. You deserved so much more. You still do. I really hope you're happy."

"I am," she said—and realized that, for the first time in years, she actually meant it.

WHAT IT MEANS TO *Let Go*

I've shared the story of my betrayal and the end of my marriage. But while I share that story to help other women deal with their own broken hearts, I don't live in it every day. It doesn't hold a charge for me anymore. I have completely forgiven him.

I won't say the process was easy. But it was worth every painful moment, every tear, and every moment of fear.

I've read at least a dozen books on forgiveness. Historically, it wasn't something I was good at. I knew the basics, of course—but I didn't fully understand it until I put everything I'd learned into practice.

When I first considered forgiving my husband for what he'd done, the first thing that came to mind was, "Mal, you're letting him off the hook!" But I knew enough about forgiveness by that point to soothe my wounded inner girl. I wasn't letting him off the hook. I was letting *myself* off.

By practicing forgiveness, I was giving myself permission to move on. I was cleaning up my side of the relationship, and owning all the stuff I did to contribute to the situation. And when I stopped judging myself for my part in the situation, it was a lot easier for me to stop judging him. I can't even describe the lightness I felt when my mind was no longer bogged down with that anger and regret.

I also realized, in this process, that I had far more people than just my ex to forgive. I needed to forgive every man who had ever betrayed me, because I was still carrying those hurts, and they were hurting me in turn. I had never really done the work, the clearing at the level I was prepared to do now. I thought these men were long gone from my life because I was no longer bleeding at the mention of their names, but pieces of them were still inside me, like shrapnel, cutting me every time I moved the wrong way.

And, in the end, the person I most needed to forgive was myself. I needed to forgive my dysfunctional neediness and the desperate co-dependency that ruled my earlier relationships. When I fully faced the pain I was responsible for creating in my younger life, I started to feel compassion for how lost I truly was. I now understood that those experiences were nothing more than a mirror for the massive turmoil existing within me. My intentions were good, but my outcomes were a disaster. I created such havoc, and put other people in really uncomfortable positions.

One by one, the hooks in my heart dissolved. I had real clarity for the first time. I was the only one responsible for my own devastation, and the only one capable of reversing it. It was massively powerful.

Today, I am on good terms with my ex-husband. I have compassion for him. I often ask myself what must have happened to him as a child to create the dark, secret thoughts he acted upon when he betrayed me. Something is buried within him that is too painful to reveal, even to the people who love him most. I can recognize today that he is doing what he feels is his healing process, and I respect his choices, even if I don't always agree with them. Reciprocally, he can sense the forgiveness and unconditional love that I have now, which has opened the conversation between us once again, particularly around our spiritual practices. I have also been able to maintain good relationships with my treasured stepchildren and grandchildren.

Forgiveness isn't a one-and-done exercise. It's a process of unraveling, to be done at your own pace, when you are ready.

Here are a few of the steps I have used myself, and suggested to my clients. Many have experienced huge transformation from these practices. I know you will as well.

FORGIVENESS PRACTICES

- Set an intention to find resolution in the situation. This is for your healing. Commit to doing this for yourself.

- Ask yourself, "When I find forgiveness, how will I feel, in my body, mind, and heart?"

- Write a letter to the person you are forgiving (even if that person is yourself). Why are you still feeling so much hurt and anger?

- Ask yourself, "Are my feelings realistic at this time? Or are they rooted in the past and my old story?"

- Let go of your opinions and judgments about the behavior that caused your anger and pain. The fact is, you don't know everything, so stop making assumptions. Ask yourself, "What would happen if I let go of thinking I've been wronged?"

- Pray and ask for healing, and for the highest and best for both of you. Ask for help to cut the cords that are keeping you tied to your pain. Visualize those old cords falling away from your body.

- Trust the process. Know that it will unfold gracefully, and that it has a higher purpose for both of you. When you are proactive for a peaceful closure, it empowers you and gives you clarity about you and what options you have. It's no longer about being right, it's about being happy again.

The feeling of forgiveness will not be instantaneous, but you will feel so much lighter as time progresses. Staying in the present moment with your thoughts and feelings will take you out of the painful trauma of your past. The more aware you become, the easier it is to stop retelling the old story. You have the ability to make different choices now; you no longer need to live as a victim to someone else's behavior. You can have harmony in your life again.

About a year ago, I met a woman named Laurie at a conference. I could sense right away that we had a lot in common; I could see it in her eyes.

There was a story behind her smile. We had an instant camaraderie.

Naturally, the conversation turned to our relationships. She was (and still is) married. But it had hardly been all wine and roses.

Harry is her second husband, and they'd been married for about five years when she sat down to their shared computer to do a Google search for gardening tools. She discovered that Harry had been doing some searching of his own. A lengthy list of dating sites scrolled out before Laurie's stunned eyes.

That was only the beginning. Turns out, Harry had been pursuing other women, and had even slept with a woman they both knew from church.

"He used to like to tell me, 'I'm doing God's work, Laurie.' I thought, 'You're doing a hell of a job, Harry.'"

She and Harry went to their pastor for counseling, and to talk through Harry's indiscretions. I have to hand it to her: her religious beliefs kept her strong.

"How did you get through it?" I asked.

"Mal, I know one thing: God didn't ask him to do what he did, but He probably did forgive him."

Laurie and Harry are still together. They've worked through their issues, and seem to be very happy. I have the greatest respect for her capacity to forgive. She has chosen to trust, because trusting lets her have a more joyful life.

***

I think you see what forgiveness can do. It can heal shattered hearts, mend old wounds, and in some cases make a relationship even stronger. All of us are flawed in some way; no one is perfect. Forgiveness reminds us, as we forgive others, that we too are in need. We can lessen the expectations we put on others and love them for who they are, instead of who we want them to be. Most importantly, forgiveness allows you to see the truth about who you are, and expand your capacity for love.

SELF-REALIZATION QUESTIONS

- What does forgiveness mean to you?

- What do you think would happen if you forgave the one who broke you open?

- If you don't feel ready to forgive, what would help you get there?

CHAPTER TWELVE

YOUR NEW HEART'S DESIRE

CHAPTER TWELVE

YOUR NEW HEART'S DESIRE

"It's not up to you what you learn, but only whether you
learn through joy or through pain."
— A Course In Miracles

*N*ow that you have done the work of healing your broken heart and absorbing the lessons of your deepest wounds, it's time to step out of your box and into a new life as a whole, healing woman.

As we discussed at the beginning of this book, there's a universal energy out there which is part of you, and which is all around you. If you want to co-create with this energy, you need to get very deliberate and intentional. You can't just say, "Oh, good! That giant shit storm is behind me. Now I can get my life back to normal."

Sorry, honey. That normal is gone for you—and thank God for that!

If you applied the forgiveness practices from the previous chapter, you are now open to manifest and receive. You have cut the cords to the negative emotions and victim mentality that were blocking you before. Your inner world is ready to show up and create a new outer world reality. You're like a blank canvas.

But when things get uncertain, or feel scary, it's so tempting to just slip back into what's familiar—especially if you haven't done the deep work of releasing your pent-up feelings and rewriting your old love story. That ghastly ghost of fear will wrap itself around your ankle and trip you up, over and over. Your old perceptions will settle over your eyes like fog. If you're not paying attention, you will soon be lost again.

The key is to keep engaging with your daily practices, and keep tuning in to what your inner wisdom has to say. Write down the fears that used to control your decisions; you'll recognize which ones come from old, destructive behaviors that you no longer engage in. The more aware you are, the less likely you are to dredge up those old habits.

Another great practice to keep old habits at bay is to cultivate gratitude every single day. Gratitude is one of the most powerful practices for connecting you with real love; without fail, it will elevate your feelings and ignite appreciation. When those thoughts of fear and neediness start to surface in your consciousness, let yourself slip into gratitude. You have untethered your heart from all that has hurt and disappointed you. You have forgiven old wrongs, and are moving into a new life full of more love than you can possibly imagine. You are ready to embrace real love, not the limited love of your old stories. Each time you remind yourself of these truths, your old ways of being will have less power over you.

Here are some helpful questions to ask yourself when you are tempted to slip back into your old habits in love and life. Feel free to add your own to the list!

- How am I letting self-doubt hold me back?

- How can I express my values clearly in this situation?

- Why am I feeling insecure?

- Where am I overlooking inappropriate behavior?

- What unrealistic expectations do I have?

- How am I feeling about myself in this situation?

- What do I need to forgive?

- What would be the best outcome for everyone?

- What specific actions should I take?

- How can I listen to others with compassion and not judgment?

Every small step that you take right now to help yourself will bring you that much closer to reconnecting with love. You will know when that warm swirling energy starts to circulate through you, that you have healed the wound from being broken open. For the first time, your inner world will be in harmony with your outer experiences.

WHAT'S IN YOUR *Cake?*

The most important thing to remember as you emerge from your cocoon of healing is that your life is about you. It always has been, and always will be—even if you once pretended differently. You are the only one responsible for your healing, your happiness, and your future. The clearer you are about that right now, the better your chances for creating and maintaining a solid connection to the love inside you.

When I teach workshops, I like to ask women to think of their lives as beautiful cakes. Each of us gets to put the best ingredients into our personal cake. Some of these might be self-care, good self-esteem, success, and passion. If we use all of these ingredients, we will end up with a giant tower of deliciousness. And if we choose, we can frost that cake with a buttery-rich relationship.

The mistake I see so many women make is that they think the *relationship* is the cake, and their self-esteem and passions are the frosting. Well, you can't have frosting without a cake to put it on. Treating yourself as a glossy add-on is a recipe for disaster. However, if you have a solid foundation and many layers of goodness in your life, relationships can come and go. Their loss might be painful, and you might feel naked, but deep down you know you will survive. You can still put one foot in front of the other. And the layers of you are still just as rich and tasty.

The best tool you have right now for baking your cake is your inner wisdom. What really needs to go into your life to make it delicious? What can you actually handle at the moment without turning your batter all lumpy and hard? Pay attention to how you feel in your body. If something feels heavy, it's probably not right in this moment. (Think angel food, not flourless torte!)

As you test out your recipes, and learn to trust yourself, this will get easier. You will start to see how you can set up your life to support you, and how you can stop relying on the frosting to make everything stick together. The faith you develop in yourself as you do this will take you further toward your joy and power than any man, any job, or any supermodel body. Your happiness comes from within; remember, when your soul speaks, it speaks the truth.

WAVES OF *Change*

At the beginning of this book, I shared that your broken heart is your badge of courage. But now, your heart is well on its way to healing. You are a whole woman once again—or maybe for the first time ever. Now, your memory of your broken heart is a keepsake, like a scar or a trinket. When you look at it, you will remember your journey to healing, and you will feel gratitude as deep as the ocean. What you once thought would kill you has made you stronger. What you once thought would strand you in darkness has led you into your light. What once broke you open actually gifted you with a breakthrough.

That said, that feeling of wholeness comes in waves, especially in the beginning. So on the days when you feel like you're drowning, don't be tempted to stomp out all the new shoots of hope growing in your broken places. Instead, take an inventory to identify where there is still work to be done. Look for the missing pieces. Stay with the feeling. Be with your healing process. Ask your heart, "What are you trying to tell me today? What do I need to know? What is the reason behind this?" I keep a notebook next to my bed so that, when my questions awaken me in the middle of the night, I can write down the guidance I receive. When I read the answers in the morning, or several days later, I'm amazed at how powerful and insightful they are. Without fail, they are about bringing more love into a situation that needs it.

To help you continue to live and love as a whole woman, I encourage you to write out a set of Soul Vows. I learned about Soul Vows from a wonderful teacher named Janet Conner, who teaches Deep Soul Writing. These vows are your guideposts for living authentically. They are your boundaries, your North Star, the foundation of your existence. When you feel lost, you can come back to them; they are a wonderful way to anchor yourself to your truth.

MY SOUL VOWS ARE:

- I shine my light to inspire others.
- I live as a reflector of truth.
- I show kindness to myself and others.
- I am an energy field of love for myself and others.
- I surrender to God's will.
- I use my heart as my guide.
- I am grateful for all I receive.

These seven vows actually encompass everything I have tried to teach you in this book and I encourage you to integrate them into your daily life. They will help you live your life as the best and most beautiful expression of you, connected to your truth and able to receive all the love and riches you deserve.

When life becomes deeply challenging, it's easy for you

to forget what really holds your life and heart together. I know this firsthand. Most of my previous vows to myself I broke in one way or another. But my Soul Vows are forever. They are the threads that hold me together. They are the assurance of what is right for me. When I read them, I feel like I can breathe again, tap into my inner wisdom, and make a decision that comes from my heart, not my head.

YOU ARE A *Magnet* FOR YOUR HEART'S DESIRE

You, my sweet, have become a magnet for your heart's desire. Now it is time to put the vision out there and let the Universe go to work on your behalf.

You have stepped through the veils of shame, self-doubt, and insecurity to reclaim your sovereignty. Now, it's time to claim what it is that you desire—whether that's a new way of living, a new vocation, or a new love like some of the women I have told you about. You can use visualizations, affirmations, or your written words. (I find that writing things down creates much more momentum for attracting what I want.)

Take fifteen minutes every morning to write in your journal detailed descriptions of your heart's desires and how you want them to show up in your life. Be as detailed as possible to create a vivid picture. These visions will contain golden nuggets of truth—the things you need to live in harmony and feel inspired. Chances are, they will align perfectly with your Soul Vows.

So get out your journal, grab a cup of tea (or a glass of wine), sit quietly, and ask yourself, "What must I absolutely have in my life?" I'm not talking about material things, but

qualitative spiritual and emotional feelings and experiences. What makes you get out of bed every day? What are your biggest values? What do you want to be remembered for? Have fun with this. Write out your answers. (Also, if you really want to go deeper into this, I can't recommend Janet Conner's book, *Soul Vows*, strongly enough.)

I read my Soul Vows every morning. It is just another way of expressing to the Universe that these are must-haves for me. You can see in my vows that I am inviting greater love and kindness for myself and others; I'm not pursuing it, or asking that it be provided to me. Everything I need is already inside of me.

Loving as a whole woman means loving your life. You might choose to invite a new partner into your sphere at this point. Or, you might invite new opportunities for travel, adventure, learning, and sharing. You might discover new ways to love your family and friends, and help them see the greatness in themselves. You might tap into your purpose for being here on Earth. It doesn't matter what you choose to create, only that it comes from your soul and supports the vows you've made to yourself. You no longer need to compromise anything about yourself for anyone.

Nothing can match the power you feel when you know, beyond a shadow of a doubt, that you are worthy, whole, and lovable. From this glorious place, you can create new relationships, a new career, or anything else you want. You are a whole woman, and the world is yours for the taking!

SELF-REALIZATION QUESTIONS

- When was the last time you thought about what you really want?

- Write out your Soul Vows. How does it feel to see your deepest values laid out so clearly?

- What is one thing you can do today to live more in alignment with your Soul Vows?

- What are you creating in your life with your daily visualizations?

CHAPTER THIRTEEN

LOVING AS A WHOLE WOMAN

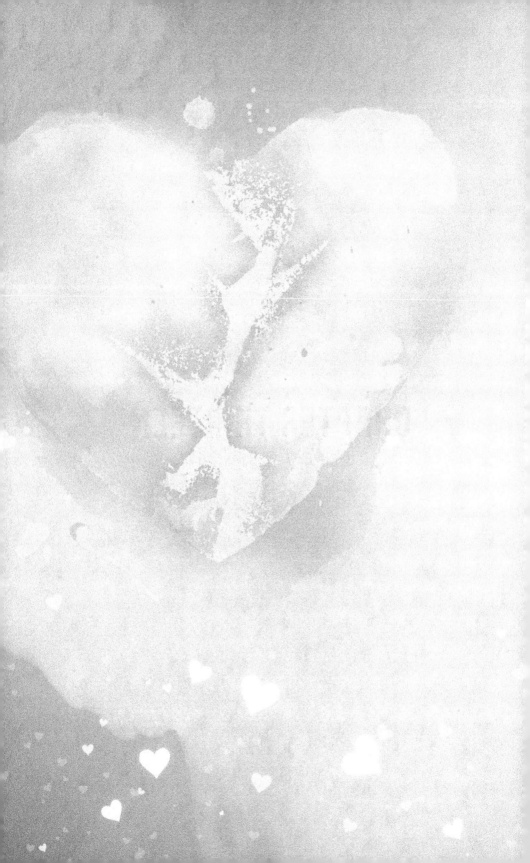

CHAPTER THIRTEEN

LOVING AS A WHOLE WOMAN

"The right way to wholeness is made up of fateful
detours and wrong turnings." - *Carl Jung*

*J*ust days before their thirtieth wedding anniversary, my
client Sandra's husband asked for a divorce because he was
in love with someone else, a younger woman. (I know, we've
all heard this story before. I wish men could come up with
something more original.) Sandra was devastated, of course.
She was numb. When we first connected, she couldn't eat or
sleep, and the intense stress of her situation was taking a huge
toll on her physical, mental, and emotional health. She was at
the end of an abyss; a few more steps toward the edge, and she
would lose her footing completely.

Sandra and I looked closely together at the steps she needed
to take to come to terms with her husband's betrayal. First, she
needed to get through her initial ego response of feeling unworthy
and having been "replaced" in her relationship because she

wasn't a twenty-something-year-old hottie anymore. She also needed to look at her love story, which was telling her, "Once a woman 'lets herself go,' her man will leave her for someone younger, fitter, and more attractive."

Next, we looked at what part of her betrayal she could own, and which parts were all on her ex. This betrayal wasn't about how Sandra looked. It was about her husband's overblown midlife crisis and his doubts about his image and sexual prowess. Maybe Sandra had "let herself go" a bit, but that wasn't what caused the betrayal. It only caused *her* to feel like she deserved the betrayal.

After her divorce was finalized, Sandra committed to freeing her heart from pain. She went into deep forgiveness. She used her morning journaling practice, breathwork, and meditation to begin to get her mind and heart back into alignment. She started exercising and eating better, so she could feel at home in her body again—not because of what her ex had done, but so that she would feel more positive about herself. She came, over the course of several months, to a place where she felt nothing but love for herself when she looked in the mirror.

When his young lover left him, Sandra's ex came crawling back asking for another chance. She felt nothing but compassion for him. She knew the pain and humiliation he must be going through. But she also knew, now, her own value. And so she followed her heart and her gut, which were telling her, "There's something more for you. You deserve more."

Because she'd done such deep healing work around repairing and rewriting her love story—taking responsibility for herself, her life, and her emotions, and forgiving her ex for betraying her—she was brilliantly happy for the first time in her life. And when that little voice inside her spoke about "something more," she decided to listen. It was time to think about attracting love again.

Sandra wrote in her journal daily about the love she would like to meet. She was specific about all of the details—his height, weight, hair and eye color, profession, likes and dislikes … you name it, she listed it. Most of all, though, she wrote about how she would like this new love to feel. When she was with this new love, she would feel more herself, more empowered, and more alive—not less. She didn't need this love for self-validation or self-completion; she wanted this love simply because she knew her already wonderful life would feel even better if she had someone to share it with.

She ended each daily journaling session with the prayer, "May the Universe deliver this or something better!"

Within six months, the Universe served up George. He was everything on her list and more. He loved that she knew what she wanted, and that she took responsibility for herself and her feelings. More, he admired her honesty, her willingness to be open, and her firm boundaries. He didn't need to be needed; he wanted to be loved, and love in return.

Together, George and Sandra have created a healthy intimate relationship where they feel mutually valued. I'm happy to report that, four years in, they are still a very hot item!

It's not someone else's job to complete you, fulfill you, or make you happy. You need to do that on your own before you can bring that completeness into a relationship. I know you've heard the adage, "You have to learn to love yourself before someone else can love you," and it's absolutely true. If you can't be happy on your own, you won't be fully happy in love.

YOU ARE *Whole* AGAIN

I hope you realize by now that you are not some self-improvement project, but a whole, self-empowered woman. You've rewritten your love story. You've taken responsibility for your part in your broken heart. You've done the work to forgive the past so you can move on and become more than you have ever been before. You've stepped into your power in a whole new way, and the road is clear in front of you.

The threads of self-love have stitched together the fragments of your heart. The place where you were broken open is no longer a gaping wound, but a sunlit valley full of new growth and blooming flowers. You have found your way out of the darkness, and the light of real love—the love that comes from within—is even more brilliant than you imagined. Your heart is whole, even though its landscape has changed, and it's pointing the way toward a fantastic new life.

The new you is on fire. She:

- No longer dwells in victim energy or blame.

- Claims her broken heart as a badge of courage.

- Surrenders to what is, instead of wishing things were different.

- Leans into her pain, instead of dismissing or denying it.

- Knows herself as a powerful feminine being capable of bringing forth love from within.

- Doesn't avoid or escalate conflict, but instead leads from her inner wisdom.

- Greets each day with intention and excitement.
- Knows that she is worthy of love, and loves herself unconditionally.

For me, going through the hot mess that was the end of my marriage opened me up to my own resiliency and capacity for love. For the first time in many, many years, my heart and head are in true alignment. I know what I want, and I own it. I don't put unrealistic pressure on myself—but I don't let myself get away with offering less than my best, either.

Every day, I wake up grateful for all that I have. I value my beautiful home, and I take really good care of it. I value my body, and I take even better care of it. I love my work, and the joy I get from helping women walk their own path to healing. I love my friends, who have walked beside me. I love my family, including my stepchildren and grandchildren, and know that our relationships are strong and positive. My life feels full.

When I run into people I haven't seen in a while, they tell me how much happier I seem. They tell me that I look better than ever, that my skin and eyes glow, and that I seem full of joy. It's amazing what peace of mind can do for you! All the emotional blocks have been lifted; now, I experience my life from a calm, centered core that is wrapped in self-worth. I will never go back to my old way of living again.

Feeling so complete and whole has also allowed me to interact with my ex on an entirely new level. My thoughts are not buried in betrayal any longer. I can laugh and joke with him like we did once upon a time—and at the same time, know that he has no power over me, and that I am not subject to him, his needs, or his values in any way. I am emotionally safe. I only allow what feels comfortable to me to transpire. Honestly, I think he might have the same feeling; I do know that he enjoys the freedom he now has to work on his own process.

Your broken heart propelled you to change your unconscious, destructive love story. It taught you to take responsibility, to become aware of what was happening inside you. It taught you to forgive, and to love yourself beyond anything you could have previously imagined.

SELF-LOVING *Boundaries*

As we explored in the last chapter, when you start drawing new opportunities, adventures, and possibly love relationships into your life, the first thing you'll notice is that they will test you. They'll tempt you to go back to your old love story, your old ways of being. They'll make you uncomfortable.

Don't give in to the temptation to go back to your old self! You're uncomfortable because you've stepped into a new paradigm. Just keep sticking to those vows, girl, and see it through.

My client Joanne is the most self-respecting woman I've ever met. (Bless her parents for instilling such confidence and self-worth in her when she was younger. Most of us have to learn it later in life!) She isn't a raving beauty, but she's attractive because of her confidence and energy. She's the woman who makes the room stop and stare when she walks in.

Men gravitate to Joanne in a way I've never seen before. They're like bees to honey. They fall over themselves to talk to her. But she never lets the attention she receives compromise her boundaries. When a man (or anyone else) does something to annoy her, or crosses a line that she's drawn for herself, she lets him know that this is unacceptable. She'll give him a chance to change, but if it happens again, it's a deal-breaker. She never allows herself to feel pressured sexually, and never lets anyone make claims on her time beyond what she decides is appropriate. There's no stuffing her feelings while she tries to figure it all out. There's no quiet withdrawal so the man can "figure it out." She puts it all on the table—and men jump through hoops to be with her.

Joanne came to me because she wanted help to manifest a long-term relationship. "I'm great on my own," she said. "But I would love to find the right person to share my life with." She wanted to meet someone who wouldn't just respect her boundaries, but actually align with them. When she started doing the morning exercises I've described in this book, she tapped into her already strong powers of discernment even more deeply. Soon, she started meeting men who were more aligned with what she wanted. She's confident that, very soon, her twin flame will appear; when he does, she'll be ready—and in the meantime, she's still not taking shit from anyone.

You have all the keys to live with as much discernment as Joanne. You are the queen of "loving smart." Just keep sticking to your values, being honest with yourself, and leaning into the learning that your beautiful broken heart has brought you.

LOVE Smart

So, what does "love smart" in the flip love language of Mal mean? It means protecting yourself from getting your ass handed to you on a silver platter again!

All kidding aside, being love smart means being consciously aware of your behavior and expressed needs in any relationship—including the one you have with yourself. If you have followed the suggestions I have given you so far, you are on the cusp of becoming love smart.

A girl who loves smart has asked the right questions and paid attention to the answers. She has listened to her intuition. She knows what is true for her in the here and now, and what is her old false love story coming through once again. She builds everything in her life on a foundation of trust. She looks within to her inner sanctuary for answers, because she knows that's where truth—and true love—come from.

When you are in the midst of a challenge, ask yourself, "Am I being love smart?" Tap into your higher self for accurate guidance. You will know if the answers you get are accurate if they are based in love, kindness, compassion, and the highest good of all. If you're hearing answers that call for aggression or unkind behavior, or which make you feel small, unworthy, or unloved, you will know that your ego is speaking, and you need to go deeper to access your divine guidance. When you are listening to the love within you, you will never be instructed to strike out in order to resolve a difference. Higher guidance doesn't create wounds, it heals them.

When you lean into love, you become a gladiator. You step into one of life's most challenging arenas. Last time you were in this space, you got your heart pierced with a sharp sword of betrayal and deceit. But now, you've healed those wounds, and you wear your scars with pride.

Being love smart means that the next time you go into the arena, you will be better equipped. You will have a stronger shield and a deeper awareness. Becoming a great gladiator in the arena of love takes practice and emotional maneuverability—and that starts with faith in yourself. You need to know what you are capable of. When you feel like you're face-down in the dirt, do you trust yourself to get up and get moving again? Or will you lay there and let that be your ending?

There's a self-assuredness that comes with being prepared. When you define early on in any situation what you actually want, what is acceptable to you, and what will actually work for you, the Universe will deliver. You give consent when a situation is in alignment with your vision and values. If it's not, you can express yourself gracefully to establish a boundary that works. You can still be flexible when things don't go as planned, but your Soul Vows won't change—and you won't tolerate anything that violates them, even from yourself. You have done so much inner work to be comfortable and authentic in who you are; now, you won't compromise that for anyone or anything.

When you're love smart, you know how to be compassionate when dealing with the weaknesses and fears of others. You appreciate people for their courage to be transparent to you. You admire another's honesty because you recognize you're not without your own flaws. If a situation does not work out as you had hoped, you are capable of forgiving other people. You don't need to feel that you are right, and they are wrong, because you aren't relying on them to give you the things that matter most (like love and self-respect). Instead, you forgive, let go, and move on.

SPARKLE AND *Shine*

For many years when I was modeling, people looked at my photographs and told me I looked great. However, if you look closely, you can see that my eyes are dark, almost flat. There is no sparkle in their depths. That's because I had no self-worth, no sense of anything else for myself. I didn't know that I had access to all the love I needed within myself.

These days, I have that sparkle in my eyes. People actually notice it and comment on it frequently. I'm living, sparkling proof that you can transform your life by having unconditional love for yourself. Having self-love is not about being selfish; it's about treating yourself well and expecting others to do the same.

Because you have done the practices suggested in this book, I know your eyes sparkle just like mine do. You've found and nurtured a real sense of self-worth. The days of belittling and condemning yourself are over. You, dear girl, can look in the mirror and love what you see. That aura of self-love will become your greatest magnet for truly fulfilling relationships, experiences, and adventures.

You are now a woman who lives with purpose. You know that within you is a unique gift you can use to serve others. You radiate love from the inside out. That is more attractive than any outfit you can put on. Everything you do is impacted by how you feel about *you*. The way you walk into a room, shake hands, or introduce yourself. That indescribable light in your eyes comes not from a reflection, but from deep in your heart.

When you love yourself as a whole woman, you attract so many more people into your life. They feel that glorious energy that surrounds you, and it works like a magnet, drawing them to you. You deserve this love and attention—but always remember, real love doesn't come from your admirers. It comes from within you.

You are now ready to cross the bridge into the life you have always wanted—a place where you are valued for your authentic self. There is no need for pretense or unhealthy compromises any longer. You are connected to your own heart like never before. You are a woman standing in her own power, knowing her value, and wearing her badge of courage. You're proud because you've made your hero's journey; you got back up when life knocked you down, and now there is nothing anyone else can take away from you without your permission. The love you feel for yourself is your guiding light.

SELF-REALIZATION QUESTIONS

- What does "loving as a whole woman" mean to you?

- How does it feel to know your boundaries and lovingly enforce them?

- Where do you feel strong at this moment? Where do you think you need more practice?

- When you look at your eyes in the mirror, do you see the sparkle of love in them?

CHAPTER FOURTEEN

A LIFETIME OF UNCONDITIONAL LOVE

CHAPTER FOURTEEN
A LIFETIME OF UNCONDITIONAL LOVE

"But at the end, if we are brave enough to love, if we
are strong enough to forgive, if we are generous enough
to rejoice in another's happiness, and if we are wise
enough to know that there is enough love to go around
for us all, then we can achieve a fulfillment that no other
living creature will ever know. We can reenter paradise."
- Rabbi Harold Kushner

*W*ell, beautiful, you have walked through the valley of
emotional death, and you are ready to traverse the mountain
of love once again. It has probably been a challenging journey
for you—but also a rewarding one. You have taken the pain of
your broken heart and reforged yourself as a powerful, divine
feminine soul. You have learned some of the biggest lessons
you need to master in this lifetime; now, you can lead the way
for other women to do their own healing and discover the truth
about the love within themselves.

Everything you do in your life leads you to a specific place.
Your current reality is an accumulation of your actions. As you
keep working with the healing techniques and actions in this
book, you will start to notice your reality changing. Nothing was
ever being done *to* you; it was all happening *through* you. You
stepped out of the darkness and into your soul's illumination.

Glorious girl, a new life of love is just around the corner for you. Where once you were curled up in a ball of pain, you are now radiating love like a beacon. Because you are shining so brightly, you will begin to attract love from all sides, in all kinds of relationships. This time, you will choose wisely for yourself, because you are whole, and standing on level ground. You will love smart!

Your job from now on is to tap into that love within you every single day. Your inner work doesn't stop when your wounds are healed over. In fact, from there, it's only beginning. Your heart is now your guiding light. You have learned the healing power of love. Now, it's your job to be consistent with your self-care and personal growth. When you feel fear trying to creep back into your heart, stop, get quiet, and listen to your body. Breathe deeply into any discomfort, and remember that love is your inner superpower. Trust yourself and your intuition, and act accordingly.

Your job on this planet is to give and receive love. The only thing that can get in the way of that is you. You can choose to live from your heart every day, and set aside your nagging ego and self-criticism. Don't let the world tell you what you need; you already know your truth. This is a continual path of surrender. Building your capacity for love, compassion, forgiveness, and gratitude will bring you far greater rewards than the right dress or the right man.

It will be your choice, from now on, to remember that your self-worth is deeper and more expansive than any hurt or victimhood. You can walk through the fires of hell and come out whole and radiant. There is no armor more powerful than your love for yourself. You can deflect, with love and grace, anything that is thrown at you. You are free from the energetic drain of judgment and condemnation.

Your future depends on how you choose to remember all of this. You will live in wholeness by knowing your own weaknesses. The desires that led you astray before are no longer controlling your heart, but if they resurface, speak to them gently. Assure them that you've got this; there is nothing to fear. After all, you're a woman who has been broken open to uncover her own strengths and magical contributions as an unending force of unconditional love.

My dear sister, walk in the light that is meant to guide you. Trust your heart, for it will never deceive you. Live your life in love and not the need to defend it. Be grateful for every minute, every lesson. Every painful moment was there to awaken you to more of your own greatness and purpose. The journey isn't always easy, but it is *so* worth it!

We will continue this journey together with greater understanding for one another. I hold you in my heart, and I want you to know that you are truly loved. We are all playing in a field of cosmic love where we become one. The light that came shining through our broken hearts has connected all of us in unconditional love.

You are no longer an ordinary woman, but a warrior for love. You have been given a shining badge of courage and a far greater capacity to love. Wear it with pride! I am celebrating you.

Your soul sister,

Mal

MAL'S LIBRARY OF LOVE

RESOURCES FOR REWRITING YOUR LOVE STORY

When I started my journey toward wholeness and healing, I found great comfort in many of the books I read and audio programs to which I listened. I often suggest these resources to other women who I meet along the way. So, for many years, I've been keeping and expanding a list of my favorites!

I've selected the following resources from my larger "Library of Love" because I think they are crucial to the journey you're on. I hope they will be helpful and enlightening for you, and aid you in your journey of personal discovery.

- *Judgment Detox: Release the Beliefs That Hold You Back from Living A Better Life* by Gabrielle Bernstein

- *The Lotus and the Lily, Access the Wisdom of Buddha and Jesus to Nourish Your Beautiful, Abundant Life* by Janet Conner

- *Find Your Soul's Purpose: Discover Who You Are, Remember Why You Are Here, Live a Life You Love* by Janet Conner

- *Soul Vows: Gathering the Presence of the Divine In You, Through You, and As You* by Janet Conner

- *Ho'oponopono: The Hawaiian Forgiveness Ritual as the Key to Your Life's Fulfillment* by Ulrich Duprée

- *Skinny, Fat, Perfect: Love Who You See In The Mirror* by Laura Fenamore

- *Boundless Love: Transforming Your Life with Grace and Inspiration* by Miranda Holden

- *Playing Big: Practical Wisdom for Women Who Want to Speak Up, Create, and Lead* by Tara Mohr

- *Anatomy of the Spirit: The Seven Stages of Power and Healing* by Caroline Myss

- *Prayer and the Five Stages of Healing* by Ron Roth, PhD

- *The Power of Now: A Guide to Spiritual Enlightenment* by Eckhart Tolle

ACKNOWLEDGMENTS

& GRATITUDES

I have been truly blessed with a support team who helped me birth this book. To me, they are my "book doulas." I had a message burning deep within my heart that I felt needed to be shared with women—a message that confirmed that women are not defined by their relationship status or by the behaviors of their loved ones. The idea kept me up at night and I would jot down notes in the dark.

Through the brilliance of my editor Bryna Haynes, all those notes and burning desires have been brought forth in *Broken Open*. Organizing so many ideas is not an easy task. Without Bryna's skillful craft, you would not be holding my new baby today. She held my hand and guided me to speak my deepest truth in this work of love; with her help, the words just flowed from my heart, so they could reach yours.

When I published my first book, *Alpha Chick*, in 2012, I met the extraordinary Linda Joy, founder of Inspired Living Publishing and *Aspire Magazine*. The light of our souls entwined into a sistership committed to serving and empowering women. Linda has been my deepest source of encouragement over the years and has held me in sacred space

when I couldn't help myself. She believes wholeheartedly in my work and in my writing. Of course, she was the natural choice to be my publisher/midwife for *Broken Open*. We spent many hours talking about the healing message I wanted to bring to women whose hearts had been broken open by love. We both knew there was a process of healing, of embracing the pain in order to become whole, that hadn't really been written about before. Linda and I have both walked this path in our lives, and emerged from our broken-openness into the divinely powerful women we are today.

The magical cover of this book, which captures the essence of your light coming back to you through the break in your heart, is the angelic graphic design of Rachel Dunham, founder of Your Brand Therapy. She swaddled my baby with tender loving care. She heard my words and translated them into this image of a shattered heart birthing a powerful healing light. My dreams of what this book would look like have become my reality. My eyes fill with tears when I hold it close to me.

I birthed this beautiful baby with the help of my doulas.

And now, I get to share her with you.

A GIFT *for You*

Download Your

BROKEN Open
GUIDED JOURNAL

www.MalDuaneCoach.com/journal-gift

ABOUT THE AUTHOR

MAL DUANE

MAL DUANE is a certified Spiritual, Professional, and Life Coach. She is also a certified Law of Attraction Practitioner. She has been recognized as a leading expert on self-worth, and is the award-winning, #1-best-selling author of *Alpha Chick: Five Steps for Moving from Pain to Power,* as well as a contributing author to the international best-selling *Inspiration for a Woman's Soul: Choosing Happiness.* She has been featured on Fox News, *Huffington Post*, ThriveGlobal.com, *Middlesex News*, *Aspire Magazine* and *Healthy Living.* She has been interviewed over 250 times on CBS Radio, Blogtalk Radio, and other media platforms on the power of choice and personal transformation for women.

Having triumphed over devastating life challenges—including the implosion of her marriage—Mal uses the lessons she has learned to coach other women and help them to reclaim their self-worth. Her life experiences of betrayal, failed relationships, depression, and recovering from alcoholism as a young woman, have provided her with extensive hands-on, in-the-trenches experience for taking hold of life and bringing forward the potential that lies buried beneath our scars and hurts.

Mal lives with her English Jack Russell Terrier, Hannah, in Framingham, Massachusetts, where she works, writes, speaks, and supports women in embracing their power and living their truth. Learn more about Mal and her work at **www.MalDuaneCoach.com**.

INSPIRED LIVING PUBLISHING

Founded in 2010 by Inspirational Catalyst, radio show host, and *Aspire Magazine* Publisher Linda Joy, Inspired Living Publishing (ILP) is an international best-selling inspirational boutique publishing company dedicated to spreading a message of love, positivity, feminine wisdom, and self-empowerment to women of all ages, backgrounds, and life paths. Linda's multimedia brands reach over 44,000 subscribers and a social media community of over 24,000 women.

Through our highly-successful anthology division, we have brought eight books and over 300 visionary female authors to best-seller status. Our powerful, high-visibility publishing, marketing, and list-building packages have brought these authors—all visionary entrepreneurs, coaches, therapists, and health practitioners—the positive, dynamic exposure they need to attract their ideal audience and thrive in their businesses.

Inspired Living Publishing also publishes single-author books by visionary female authors whose messages are aligned with Linda's philosophy of authenticity, empowerment, and personal transformation. Recent best-selling releases include the collaborative book, *SHINE! Stories to Inspire You to Dream Big, Fear Less & Blaze Your Own Trail*; *Soul-Hearted*

Living: A Year of Sacred Reflections & Affirmations for Women by Dr. Debra Reble; *Everything Is Going to Be Okay!: From the Projects to Harvard to Freedom* by Dr. Catherine Hayes, CPCC; *Awakening to Life: Your Sacred Guide to Consciously Creating a Life of Purpose, Magic, and Miracles* by Patricia Young; and the multiple award-winning *The Art of Inspiration: An Editor's Guide to Writing Powerful, Effective Inspirational & Personal Development Books*, by ILP Chief Editor Bryna Haynes.

ILP's family of authors reap the benefits of being a part of a sacred family of inspirational multimedia brands which deliver the best in transformational and empowering content across a wide range of platforms. Our hybrid publishing packages and *à la carte* marketing and media packages provide visionary female authors with access to our proven best-seller model and high-profile multimedia exposure across all of Linda's imprints (including *Aspire Magazine*, the "Inspired Conversations" radio show on OMTimes Radio, the Inspired Living Giveaway, Inspired Living Secrets, and exposure to Linda's loyal personal audience of over 44,000 women).

If you're ready to publish your transformational book, or share your story in one of ours, we invite you to join us! Learn more at **www.InspiredLivingPublishing.com**.

IF YOU ENJOYED THIS BOOK, VISIT

WWW.INSPIREDLIVINGPUBLISHING.COM

and sign up for ILP's e-zine to receive news about hot new releases,promotions, and information on exciting author events!

CPSIA information can be obtained
at www.ICGtesting.com
Printed in the USA
LVHW081416130920
665868LV00017B/1452

9 781732 742512